Mifflin
Harcourt

Science

Grade 5

Printed in the U.S.A.

ISBN 978-0-544-26815-9

      7 8 9 10 0982 22 21 20 19 18 17

4500651915   B C D E F G

Core Skills Science
GRADE 5
Table of Contents

Table of Contents
Core Skills Science, Grade 5

Introduction

The *Core Skills Science* series offers parents and educators high-quality, curriculum-based products that align with the Next Generation Science Standards* Disciplinary Core Ideas for grades 1–8. The *Core Skills Science* series provides informative and grade-appropriate readings on a wide variety of topics in life, earth, and physical science. Two pages of worksheets follow each reading passage. The book includes:

- clear illustrations, making scientific concepts accessible to young learners

- engaging reading passages, covering a wide variety of topics in life, earth, and physical science

- logically sequenced activities, transitioning smoothly from basic comprehension to higher-order thinking skills

- comprehension questions, ascertaining that students understand what they have read

- vocabulary activities, challenging students to show their understanding of scientific terms

- critical thinking activities, increasing students' ability to analyze, synthesize, and evaluate scientific information

- questions in standardized-test format, helping prepare students for state exams

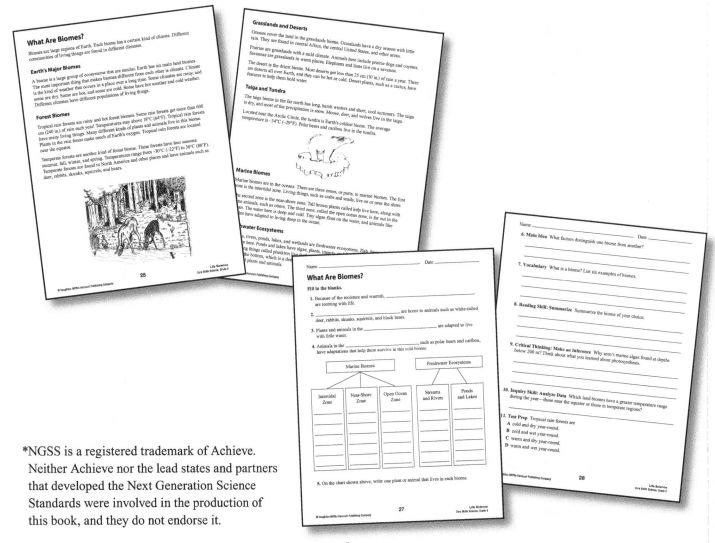

*NGSS is a registered trademark of Achieve. Neither Achieve nor the lead states and partners that developed the Next Generation Science Standards were involved in the production of this book, and they do not endorse it.

What Are the Parts of a Cell?

Cells are the basic units of living things. Tools called microscopes help scientists learn about the parts of cells and the jobs cells do.

Building Blocks of Life

The simple unit that makes up living things is the cell. All living things are made of cells. Tiny fish, people, and huge elephants are made of cells.

When you look at most living things, you cannot see their cells. That is because most cells are too small to see without a tool called a microscope. The microscope helped scientists discover cells and learn about their parts, or structures.

English scientist Robert Hooke was the first person to study cells with a microscope. He looked at dead cells in matter called cork. Dutch microscope maker Anton van Leeuwenhoek was the first person to study living cells. He saw tiny living things in a drop of water.

The Cell Theory

Over time, scientists used stronger microscopes to learn more about cells. In 1838, a German scientist looked at cells from many different plants. He learned that all plants are made of cells. Another scientist learned that all animals are made of cells. Twenty years later, a German doctor learned that cells come only from other cells.

Eventually, these ideas about cells were put together to form one scientific explanation, or theory, about cells. The cell theory says:

- All living things are made of one or more cells.
- The cell is the smallest unit of a living thing.
- Cells come from other cells.

Microscope Development

The first microscopes had one lens. The lens of a microscope collects and focuses light. Today's microscopes can make objects look 2,000 times bigger. That's powerful enough to see structures within cells. Electron microscopes use quickly moving electrons instead of light to look at objects. They can make objects look 40,000 times bigger.

The Parts of a Cell

Cells are made up of structures called organelles. Each structure has a job inside the cell. Animal and plant cells have many of the same organelles, but some are very different.

Nucleus   The nucleus directs what happens in a cell. It holds a tiny bit of matter called DNA. DNA is what makes a living thing have certain traits, or qualities.

Cell membrane   The cell membrane is a thin, bendable cover that is wrapped around all cells. It lets food, water, and gases enter the cell, and it lets wastes leave.

Cell wall   Found only in plant cells, the cell wall is a stiff outer layer around the cell membrane. The cell wall protects the cell and helps a plant stand up.

Cytoplasm   The cytoplasm is found between the nucleus and the cell membrane. All of the other organelles float in the thick liquid of the cytoplasm.

Ribosomes   Tiny ribosomes can be found all over the cell. Ribosomes make proteins.

Golgi apparatus   The Golgi apparatus takes in proteins and changes them so they are ready to leave the cell.

Lysosomes   Lysosomes are small, round organelles that help the cell break down food. Lysosomes are found in most animal cells, but they are not often found in plant cells.

Vacuoles   Vacuoles are sacs filled with liquid. They hold water, food, and waste.

Mitochondria   Mitochondria are large organelles that are shaped like peanuts. They are known as the "power plants" of the cell.

Chloroplasts   Chloroplasts are found mostly in plants. Inside chloroplasts are chemicals called pigments. The pigment called chlorophyll gives plants their green color.

Endoplasmic reticulum   The endoplasmic reticulum (ER) is a group of membranes and tubes that twist and turn through the cell, forming tunnels. Material moves through the cell in these tunnels.

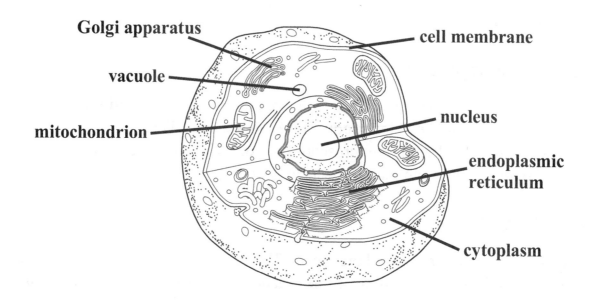

What Are the Parts of a Cell?

Write answers to the questions on the lines below.

1. What part of the cell directs the activities of the cell and stores DNA?

_____

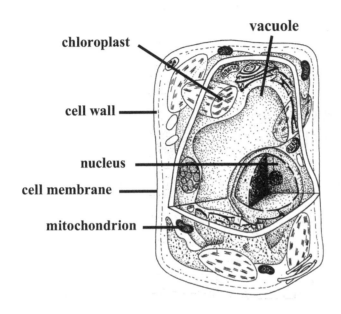

2. Is the cell above a plant cell or an animal cell? Explain how you know.

_____

_____

Match each definition to its term.

Definitions	Terms
____ **3.** thick fluid between the nucleus and the cell membrane	**a.** vacuoles
____ **4.** organelles that assemble proteins	**b.** mitochondria
____ **5.** membrane-bound sacs that are filled with fluid	**c.** cytoplasm
____ **6.** the "power plants" of the cell	**d.** ribosomes
____ **7.** a system of membranes and tubes that create passages through which materials can pass	**e.** endoplasmic reticulum

Life Science
Core Skills Science, Grade 5

8. Main Idea What are the three main points of the cell theory?

_____

_____

9. Vocabulary Write a sentence using the terms *cell* and *nucleus*. Explain the role of the nucleus in the cell.

_____

_____

10. Reading Skill: Compare and Contrast How are the uses of a light microscope and an electron microscope similar? How are they different?

_____

_____

_____

11. Critical Thinking: Evaluate How would you determine whether a cell came from an animal or a plant? Discuss cell parts.

_____

_____

_____

12. Inquiry Skill: Communicate Write a paragraph explaining how a cell membrane is similar to a cell wall. How is it different?

_____

_____

_____

13. Test Prep Which of these organelles is part of a plant cell but not an animal cell?

   A mitochondrion

   B cell membrane

   C chloroplast

   D nucleus

How Do Single-Celled Organisms Live?

In single-celled living things, or organisms, all of the actions that are needed for life happen in just one cell.

Life as a Single Cell

All living things have some of the same needs. They need to take in food and get rid of wastes. They need to break down food to use and store energy. They also need to grow and reproduce, or have offspring. These needs are called life processes. Single-celled organisms carry out all of their life processes in one cell.

You can see most single-celled organisms only with a microscope. Because of this, they are called microorganisms. Bacteria, which can sometimes make you sick, are one kind of microorganism.

Yeasts are useful microorganisms. Mixed with other ingredients, including water and sugar, yeast produces carbon dioxide gas. The expanding gas bubbles cause bread and pizza dough to rise.

Interactions with Larger Organisms

Single-celled organisms are everywhere. Helpful single-celled bacteria break down dead animals and plants. Bacteria also help to make foods such as yogurt and cheese. In fact, your body needs some kinds of bacteria to break down, or digest, foods.

Other bacteria can make you sick when they enter your body. Antibiotics are medicines that kill harmful bacteria without hurting the good cells in your body.

Algae and yeasts are other helpful single-celled organisms. Like plants, algae give off oxygen, which goes into the air, allowing you to breathe.

Getting Food

All organisms need energy. Some make their own food. Others take in or eat food from the outside.

Single-celled organisms get food in different ways. An amoeba stretches itself around food, making a bag, or vacuole, around the food. The food is digested and then taken into the cytoplasm.

A paramecium gets food in a different way. Its body has a space called an oral groove. Small hairs called cilia move around the opening of the oral groove, pushing pieces of food inside.

Diffusion

Some things move through the organism's cell membrane. One way this happens is through diffusion. Diffusion is the movement of particles from an area crowded with particles to an area where there are fewer particles. Osmosis is diffusion in which water passes through the cell membrane.

Movement

Some single-celled organisms can move from place to place, like animals do.

The amoeba moves by pushing its cell membrane in front of it. This forms a pseudopod, or "false foot."

The paramecium moves by using its hairy cilia. The cilia move back and forth, like oars on a boat.

Another single-celled organism, the euglena, has a long structure that moves back and forth quickly. This structure is called a flagellum.

Reproduction

Organisms must produce more of their kind so their group of organisms, or species, stays alive. They do this through reproduction. Single-celled organisms reproduce in different ways.

Bacteria reproduce in a simple way called binary fission. Every cell has genetic information—information about itself—inside of it. Before a parent cell reproduces, it grows longer and makes a copy of its genetic information. Next, the cell breaks apart in the middle to form two new cells.

Budding is another type of reproduction. In budding, a small bump, or bud, forms on a parent cell. The bud has the same genetic information as the parent cell. When the bud grows larger, it breaks off from the parent cell.

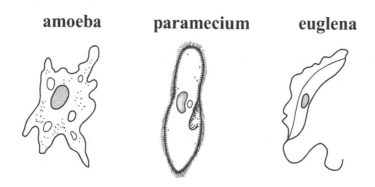

amoeba   paramecium   euglena

How Do Single-Celled Organisms Live?

Write answers to the questions on the lines below.

1. Like all living things, single-celled organisms carry out which life processes?

   _____

   _____

2. What are ways that bacteria are helpful?

   _____

   _____

   _____

   _____

3. What are diffusion and osmosis?

   _____

   _____

   _____

   _____

4. What type of reproduction occurs when a small bump, or bud, forms on a parent cell and then breaks off to form a new cell?

   _____

   _____

bacterium types

Organism 1

Organism 2

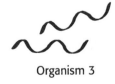

Organism 3

5. Main Idea Which needs do single-celled organisms have in common with organisms that have more than one cell?

_____

_____

6. Vocabulary Write a sentence or short paragraph using the terms *diffusion* and *osmosis*.

_____

_____

_____

7. Reading Skill: Draw Conclusions Suppose you discover a microbe that has both cilia and a flagellum. What might you conclude about the purpose of the cilia?

_____

_____

8. Critical Thinking: Apply What might happen if you take a medicine that is strong enough to kill almost all of the bacteria in your body?

_____

_____

9. Inquiry Skill: Hypothesize Do yeast need air to release carbon dioxide? Propose a hypothesis to answer this question. Describe an experiment to test it.

_____

_____

10. Test Prep Single-celled organisms use flagella, cilia, or pseudopods to

    A move from place to place.

    B break down food.

    C reproduce.

    D pump out water.

How Are Cells Organized?

Multicellular Organisms

Multicellular organisms are made up of more than one cell. In these organisms, the cells work together to keep life processes going. The cells are specialized, which means they only do certain jobs. By working together, these cells help an organism stay alive.

Cells come in many shapes and sizes. The shape of a cell often matches the job it does. Nerve cells are long and have many branches, like a tree. This shape helps them take electrical messages, or impulses, all over the body.

Cells in multicellular organisms are sorted, or organized, into different levels. The levels start out simple and get more complex.

First, cells are organized into tissues. A tissue is a large group of specialized cells that are alike. Tissue comes in many types. Muscle tissue, for example, is made of long groups, or bundles, of muscle cells.

Different types of tissues make up organs. An organ is a group of tissues that work together to do a certain job. The heart, brain, and stomach are organs.

Organs are organized into organ systems. An organ system is a group of organs that work together to do a certain job. Most multicellular organisms have a number of organ systems that come together to form the total organism.

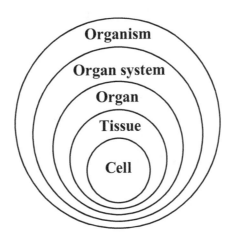

Circulatory System

The circulatory system is the organ system that brings oxygen and nutrients to all the cells in an animal's body. It also takes carbon dioxide and wastes away from the cells.

In humans and many other animals, the heart is the most important organ in the circulatory system. Arteries carry blood away from the heart. Veins carry blood back to the heart. Capillaries are tiny tubes that connect arteries to veins.

Respiratory System

The respiratory system brings oxygen to the blood and takes carbon dioxide away from it. In humans and other land animals, the lungs are the main organs in the respiratory system.

Digestive System

The digestive system breaks down, or digests, food so the body can use it. Digestion begins in the mouth, where food is chewed and mixed with liquid called saliva. The food then moves into a tube called the esophagus, on to the stomach, and into the small intestine.

Nervous System

Your nervous system controls how the body moves. Specialized cells called neurons make up the nervous system. In the brain, more than 100 billion neurons work together to help you think, remember, and learn.

Muscular and Skeletal Systems

The muscular system in the human body has three types of muscle tissue. Smooth muscles are involuntary muscles. You do not have to tell them to contract. Cardiac muscle is found only in the heart. It makes your heart beat. Skeletal muscles are voluntary muscles. You must think about moving them before they will move. Vertebrates are animals with internal skeletal systems made of bones, ligaments, and tendons. Invertebrates do not have these structures, but may have hard external shells called exoskeletons.

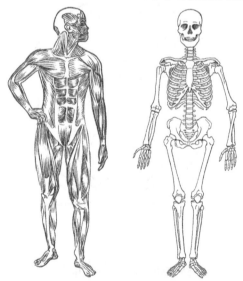

Endocrine and Excretory Systems

The endocrine system is made up of glands. Glands are organs that send chemical messages called hormones wherever the body needs them. The excretory system uses the intestines, kidneys, and even the skin to take wastes out of the body.

Name _____ Date _____

How Are Cells Organized?

Fill in the chart to show how cells are organized to make up an organism. Next to each numbered word, put a definition as shown in the example.

Cells

Example: Tissues–a large group of similar specialized cells

1. _____   _____

2. _____   _____

Organism

Match each organ system to its description.

Descriptions

Organ Systems

____ 3. brings oxygen to the blood, and removes carbon dioxide from it

____ 4. breaks down food into simpler substances

____ 5. receives and processes information and controls how the body reacts and moves

____ 6. sends chemical messages called hormones to other parts of the body

____ 7. made up of bones, ligaments, and tendons

a. nervous system

b. respiratory system

c. digestive system

d. skeletal system

e. endocrine system

8. Main Idea What functions do capillaries perform in the body?

_____

_____

9. Vocabulary Write a sentence or short paragraph using the terms *tissue* and *organ*.

_____

_____

_____

10. Reading Skill: Main Idea and Details Choose two human body organ systems. Describe the main function of each.

_____

_____

_____

11. Critical Thinking: Apply How are vertebrates and invertebrates different from each other?

_____

12. Inquiry Skill: Ask Questions Give examples of questions that scientists might ask about a cell, a tissue, an organ, an organ system, and an organism.

_____

_____

_____

13. Test Prep A major organ of the nervous system is the

    A stomach.

    B brain.

    C kidney.

    D lung.

How Do Plants Make Food?

Photosynthesis

You use energy all the time to move, work, and play. The energy you use comes from the food you eat. Food stores energy, and this energy is transferred to you when you eat it. But the energy you use originally comes from the sun. It all starts with plants. Plants use energy from the sun to make food. They do this by changing the energy of sunlight into the chemical energy stored in food. This process is called photosynthesis.

During photosynthesis, plants combine water and carbon dioxide to make sugars. They also give off oxygen. Sugars are a plant's food. The plant stores sugars in its tissues and breaks them down when it needs energy.

When an animal eats the plant, the animal can use the plant's sugars as energy. This is how all animals get their energy from plants.

Photosynthesis happens in organelles called chloroplasts. Some tiny algae cells have only one chloroplast. The cells in the leaves of a tree may each have more than fifty chloroplasts.

Most chloroplasts have the same structure. There are two thin coverings, or membranes, around each one. Another group of membranes moves inside the chloroplast. These membranes look like flat bags stacked on top of each other. They are called grana. Inside these membranes are different pigments. The most important pigment in a chloroplast is chlorophyll.

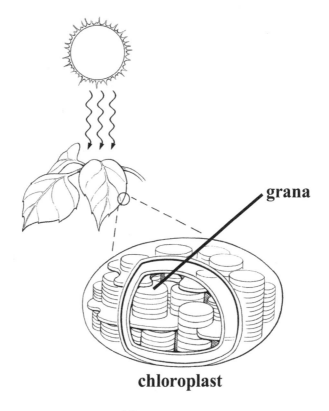

grana

chloroplast

13

Chlorophyll absorbs most colors in sunlight, but not green. When sunlight hits chlorophyll, green light is reflected back to your eye. This is why plant parts that have a lot of chlorophyll look green.

In photosynthesis, light hits chlorophyll, and the energy breaks water molecules into hydrogen and oxygen. Chemical changes make hydrogen join with carbon from carbon dioxide to form sugars. The oxygen is let go.

Plant Leaves

In most plants, leaves hold most of the chloroplasts. The wide, flat part of a leaf is called the blade. Scientists group leaves by looking at their blades. A simple leaf has a blade that is just one piece. Oak trees have simple leaves. A compound blade is separated into parts. Palm trees have compound leaves.

The outside layer of leaf tissue is called the epidermis. Small holes in the epidermis, called stomata, let gases move in and out of the plant cells. When the stomata open, carbon dioxide goes in, and oxygen and water vapor go out.

Most of the cells that help with photosynthesis can be found just below the epidermis. These cells have plenty of air in between them so gases can move easily.

Carbon and Oxygen Cycles

Oxygen and carbon dioxide cycle, or keep moving, all around us. Plants take in carbon dioxide and give off oxygen. Both plants and animals use oxygen. Together, plants and animals reuse the gases they both need, over and over.

When people burn fossil fuels such as coal and oil, carbon is sent out as carbon dioxide. People are also cutting down trees in forests. This means there are fewer trees to take carbon out of the air and send oxygen into the air.

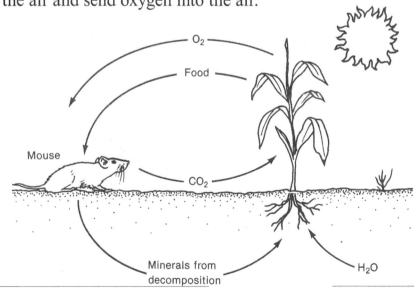

14

Name _____ Date _____

How Do Plants Make Food?

Fill in the blanks.

1. During _____, plants combine water and carbon dioxide into compounds called sugars.

2. The plant stores _____ in its tissues and breaks them down when it needs energy.

3. Photosynthesis takes place in organelles called _____.

4. Stacked membranes that contain pigment inside chloroplasts are called

    _____.

5. Plant parts that contain large amounts of _____ look green.

6. Scientists group leaves by the structure of the _____.

7. Small openings in the epidermis that allow oxygen and carbon dioxide to enter or

    leave the cells are called _____.

8. During photosynthesis, the plant keeps hydrogen molecules and releases

    _____ molecules.

9. When people burn fossil fuels, the carbon is released as

    _____.

Name _____ Date _____

10. Main Idea What are the two main products of photosynthesis?

_____

_____

11. Vocabulary Write a paragraph using the terms *chloroplast* and *stomata*. Describe the role of these structures in photosynthesis.

_____

_____

12. Reading Skill: Sequence Describe the purpose and steps of photosynthesis. Why is it important to all life on Earth?

_____

_____

13. Critical Thinking: Infer A typical cactus has a green stem and thin, spike-like needles that are not green. In which of its parts does a cactus perform photosynthesis? Explain.

_____

_____

14. Inquiry Skill: Experiment Do houseplants affect the quality of air in a house? Describe an experiment to answer this question. What gases would you want to measure?

_____

_____

15. Test Prep In leaves, what do cells just below the epidermis do?

   A Produce hydrogen gas.

   B Store nutrients.

   C Perform photosynthesis.

   D Create fossil fuels.

How Do Plants Move Materials?

Plants have specialized tissues and use natural forces to move water, minerals, and food.

Nonvascular Plants

Look at fuzzy moss growing on a tree. Not all plants look alike. Mosses are nonvascular plants. They do not have structures, or parts, like true leaves, stems, or roots. They also do not have structures to move food, water, and other things between plant parts.

Nonvascular plants are almost always small because they cannot move water very far. Most of the cells of nonvascular plants must be close to the world outside them. Gases, water, and minerals move between the outside world and the cells.

Vascular Plants

Most plants you know, including evergreen trees, ferns, and flowers, are vascular plants. A vascular plant has specialized tissues that move materials through the plant. Veins carry materials in and out of leaves. Veins are vascular tissues.

Three of the organs of vascular plants are roots, stems, and leaves. Roots hold a plant in the ground and take in water and minerals from the soil. Some roots store food for the plant.

The stem helps a plant stand up and holds its leaves up in the air so they can take in sunlight. Water, minerals, and food move from the roots to the leaves through the stem. The trunk of a tree is the tree's main stem. Stems are made of two important kinds of tissues: xylem and phloem. Xylem tissues move water and minerals up from the roots. Phloem tissues move food materials down from the leaves to the rest of the plant.

Most plant stems have a ring of bundles that contain both xylem and phloem. A strip of tissue called the vascular cambium lies between the xylem and phloem. Xylem and phloem cells are made here.

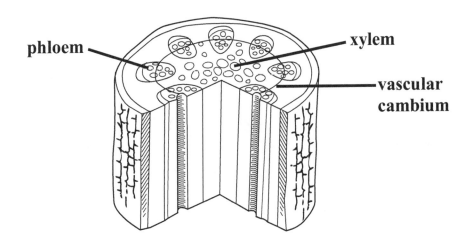

The Upward Flow of Water

In the stems of plants, water flows upward because of root pressure, cohesion, and transpiration. Water enters the roots because roots are dryer than the soil around them. Specialized cells hold water in the roots. As the roots fill with water, a force called pressure gets stronger and starts to push the water up the plant.

Water molecules and minerals stick together because of a force called cohesion. They also stick to other things because of a force called adhesion. These forces move the water up the tubes of the xylem tissue.

To reach the tops of taller plants, water needs the pull of transpiration. During transpiration, water evaporates out of the plant's leaves. As the water moves out of the leaves into the air, more water is pulled up the plant to take its place. At the same time, nutrients flow through the body of the plant.

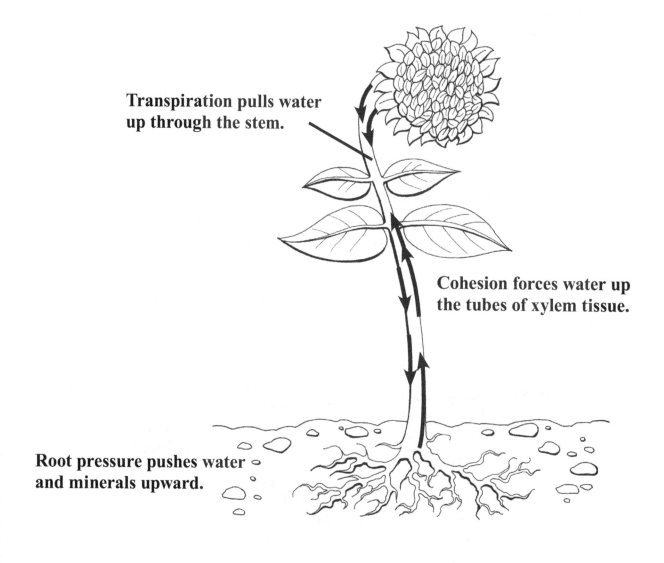

Transpiration pulls water up through the stem.

Cohesion forces water up the tubes of xylem tissue.

Root pressure pushes water and minerals upward.

Life Science
Core Skills Science, Grade 5

How Do Plants Move Materials?

Draw a line from each term to its location in the drawing.

1. roots

2. stem

3. leaves

Write answers to the questions on the lines below.

4. Which forces cause upward movement in a plant?

_____

_____

5. What is the function of the specialized cells in the outer walls of plant roots?

_____

6. How does cohesion help water and minerals to flow?

_____

_____

_____

7. Which process includes evaporation?

_____

_____

8. Main Idea How are nonvascular plants different from vascular plants?

_____

_____

9. Vocabulary Write a paragraph using the terms *xylem* and *phloem*.

_____

_____

_____

10. Reading Skill: Text Structure List three details about the vascular cambium.

_____

_____

11. Critical Thinking: Hypothesis Suppose you coated the leaves of a vascular plant with a substance that prevents transpiration. How would this affect the movement of water up the plant?

_____

_____

12. Inquiry Skill: Predict What would happen if you forgot to water the plants in your garden?

_____

_____

13. Test Prep Evaporation from plant leaves is called

   A root pressure.

   B transpiration.

   C osmosis.

   D cohesion.

How Do Plants Reproduce?

Plants reproduce using spores and seeds. The path a plant follows as it begins life, grows, and reproduces is called its life cycle. Scientists sort plants into two major groups by looking at their life cycles.

Seedless Plants and Conifers

One group is the seedless plants, which reproduce with spores or other structures. Ferns are seedless plants that reproduce with spores. Spores are made on sporangia on the back side of the fern.

The other group is the seed plants, which reproduce with seeds. Scientists sort seed plants into two large groups: gymnosperms and angiosperms. Plants with seeds that are not hidden inside of fruit are called gymnosperms. Conifers, such as pine trees, are common gymnosperms. Conifer seeds grow inside cones.

Male cones make pollen, which contains sperm cells. Female cones have ovules, which contain eggs. Pollen cones send pollen into the wind. When pollen is delivered to eggs, the process is called pollination. Sperm cells fertilize the eggs to form zygotes, which will turn into seeds.

Flowering Plants

The second group of seed plants is the angiosperms, also called flowering plants. Their seeds are protected inside flowers and fruits. Most plants in the world are angiosperms. Flowers are the organ angiosperms use for reproduction.

The male reproductive organ is called a stamen. It has a thin stalk and a rounded anther. The anther makes pollen.

The female reproductive organ of a flower is called a pistil. The pistil has three parts: the stigma, the style, and the ovary. The stigma is the sticky tip of the pistil. The style joins the stigma and ovary, which holds the ovules, or eggs. The petals of a flower protect the flower's reproductive organs.

In flowering plants, pollination happens after pollen lands on the sticky stigma. If the pollen is from the right kind of plant, the pollen makes a tube through which a sperm cell is sent to fertilize the egg. A zygote grows and turns into a seed.

As the seed grows, the ovary changes into a fruit, which keeps the seed safe. Fruits like apples and cherries are ovaries surrounding the seeds inside them.

Angiosperms grow in most places on Earth. Some even live in ocean water. Angiosperms have many kinds of structures that help them reproduce in the places they live.

Pollination

Pollen can be moved in many ways. Self-pollination occurs when pollen moves from male to female parts on the same flower. Some plants, such as corn, send pollen into the wind. Plants such as sea grasses live in water, which carries pollen. When insects and other animals visit flowers, pollen sticks on their bodies and moves with them to other flowers.

Moving Seeds Around

Like pollen, plant seeds can be moved in many ways.

Wind   Some plants, like dandelions, have small, light seeds that can be carried by the wind.

Water   Some plant seeds and fruits can be moved by water. These fruits and seeds have air inside of them to help them float in the water.

Animals   Burrs are fruits that stick to the fur of animals. As an animal moves around, it carries the seeds to new places.

Many animals like eating sweet fruits. As an animal eats the fruit, some of the seeds may drop to the ground, where they may grow into new plants.

Animals that eat fruit also help spread seeds in another way. Some seeds pass through the body of an animal without being broken down. They are part of the animal's waste. Birds that eat fruit often spread plant seeds this way.

How Do Plants Reproduce?

Match each definition to its term.

Definitions

Terms

____ 1. a plant's generation, growth, and reproduction

a. pollination

____ 2. the first cell of a new plant

b. angiosperms

____ 3. plants with seeds in cones, not covered by protective fruit

c. life cycle

d. gymnosperms

____ 4. the process that delivers pollen to eggs

e. zygote

____ 5. plants that produce seeds that have a protective covering

Use the diagram to answer questions 6, 7, and 8.

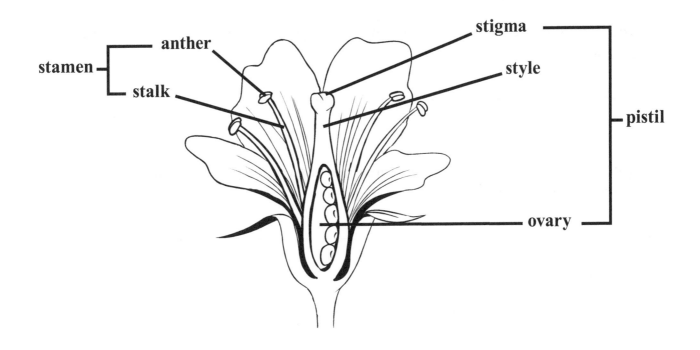

6. The male part of the flower is called the _____.

7. The female part of the flower is called the _____.

8. Pollen from the stamen reaches the _____.

23

9. Main Idea What are the most numerous types of plants?

_____

_____

10. Vocabulary Write a sentence or short paragraph using the terms *gymnosperms* and *angiosperms*.

_____

_____

_____

11. Reading Skill: Compare and Contrast What do sporangia, cones, and flowers have in common? How do they differ?

_____

_____

12. Critical Thinking: Apply Explain why many gardeners plant flowers that attract bees and butterflies.

_____

_____

13. Inquiry Skill: Analyze Data Give three reasons why angiosperms are the most dominant plants on Earth.

_____

_____

14. Test Prep All flowering plants produce seeds and

    A fruits.

    B other edible parts.

    C brightly colored petals.

    D sporangia.

What Are Biomes?

Biomes are large regions of Earth. Each biome has a certain kind of climate. Different communities of living things are found in different climates.

Earth's Major Biomes

A biome is a large group of ecosystems that are similar. Earth has six main land biomes. The most important thing that makes biomes different from each other is climate. Climate is the kind of weather that occurs in a place over a long time. Some climates are rainy, and some are dry. Some are hot, and some are cold. Some have hot weather and cold weather. Different climates have different populations of living things.

Forest Biomes

Tropical rain forests are rainy and hot forest biomes. Some rain forests get more than 600 cm (240 in.) of rain each year! Temperatures stay above 18°C (64°F). Tropical rain forests have many living things. Many different kinds of plants and animals live in this biome. Plants in the rain forest make much of Earth's oxygen. Tropical rain forests are located near the equator.

Temperate forests are another kind of forest biome. These forests have four seasons: summer, fall, winter, and spring. Temperatures range from –30°C (–22°F) to 30°C (86°F). Temperate forests are found in North America and other places and have animals such as deer, rabbits, skunks, squirrels, and bears.

Grasslands and Deserts

Grasses cover the land in the grasslands biome. Grasslands have a dry season with little rain. They are found in central Africa, the central United States, and other areas.

Prairies are grasslands with a mild climate. Animals here include prairie dogs and coyotes. Savannas are grasslands in warm places. Elephants and lions live on a savanna.

The desert is the driest biome. Most deserts get less than 25 cm (10 in.) of rain a year. There are deserts all over Earth, and they can be hot or cold. Desert plants, such as a cactus, have features to help them hold water.

Taiga and Tundra

The taiga biome in the far north has long, harsh winters and short, cool summers. The taiga is dry, and most of the precipitation is snow. Moose, deer, and wolves live in the taiga.

Located near the Arctic Circle, the tundra is Earth's coldest biome. The average temperature is –34°C (–29°F). Polar bears and caribou live in the tundra.

Marine Biomes

Marine biomes are in the oceans. There are three zones, or parts, to marine biomes. The first zone is the intertidal zone. Living things, such as crabs and snails, live on or near the shore.

The second zone is the near-shore zone. Tall brown plants called kelp live here, along with some animals, such as otters. The third zone, called the open ocean zone, is far out in the ocean. The water here is deep and cold. Tiny algae float on the water, and animals like whales have adapted to living deep in the ocean.

Freshwater Ecosystems

Streams, rivers, ponds, lakes, and wetlands are freshwater ecosystems. Fish, beavers, and birds live here. Ponds and lakes have algae, plants, insects, and fish that live near the top. Tiny living things called plankton live farther down where the water is cooler. Few things live near the bottom, which is a deep, cold area. Tiny living things called bacteria break down dead plants and animals.

Name _____ Date _____

What Are Biomes?

Fill in the blanks.

1. Because of the moisture and warmth, _____
   are teeming with life.

2. _____ are home to animals such as white-tailed
   deer, rabbits, skunks, squirrels, and black bears.

3. Plants and animals in the _____ are adapted to live
   with little water.

4. Animals in the _____, such as polar bears and caribou,
   have adaptations that help them survive in this cold biome.

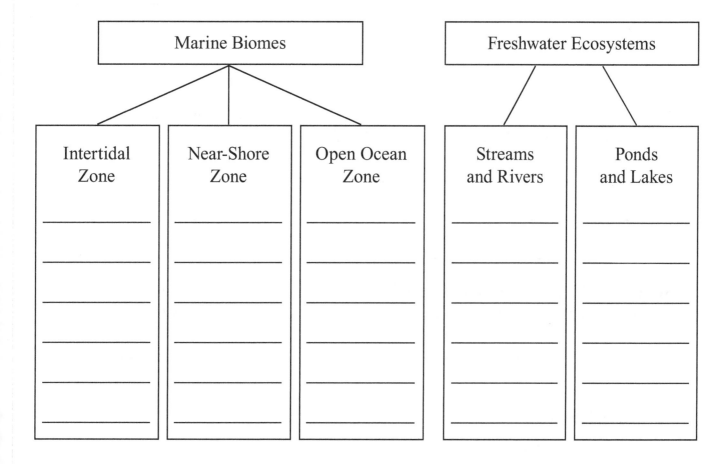

5. On the chart shown above, write one plant or animal that lives in each biome.

Life Science
Core Skills Science, Grade 5

6. Main Idea What factors distinguish one biome from another?

_____

_____

7. Vocabulary What is a biome? List six examples of biomes.

_____

_____

_____

8. Reading Skill: Summarize Summarize the biome of your choice.

_____

_____

_____

9. Critical Thinking: Make an Inference Why aren't marine algae found at depths below 200 m? Think about what you learned about photosynthesis.

_____

_____

_____

10. Inquiry Skill: Analyze Data Which land biomes have a greater temperature range during the year—those near the equator or those in temperate regions?

_____

11. Test Prep Tropical rain forests are

    A cold and dry year-round.

    B cold and wet year-round.

    C warm and dry year-round.

    D warm and wet year-round.

What Is a Food Web?

In an ecosystem, energy flows from producers to consumers to decomposers.

Energy from Food

A producer makes its own food. Plants, along with algae and some bacteria, are Earth's producers. Producers use energy from the sun. They change it into a different kind of energy made up of sugars and oxygen.

A consumer does not produce food, but gets energy by eating food. When you eat a plant, you take in energy stored in the plant. This energy is needed to stay warm, as well as to move. Humans and all other animals are consumers.

Food Chains

A food chain shows how energy in an ecosystem moves from one living thing to another. Producers make food. Animals called first-level consumers eat plants or other producers. Caterpillars are first-level consumers.

Some consumers eat other consumers. Many birds are second-level consumers. They eat very small consumers. Cats are third-level consumers. They eat larger consumers than birds do. However, without plants, there would be no food chain at all.

When plants and animals die, sometimes they are eaten. Decomposers, like bacteria, fungi, and worms, often break down parts of dead plants and animals and make them part of the soil.

Food Webs

A food web shows how food chains work in an ecosystem. A mouse might eat grass or seeds. It could also eat insects. A snake might eat insects and mice. An owl might eat mice and snakes. So could a raccoon.

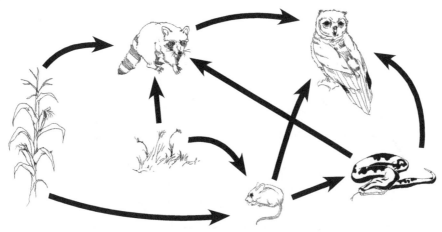

29

Life Science
Core Skills Science, Grade 5

Most consumers play the same role in every food chain they are part of. For example, a rabbit is always a first-level consumer because it is a plant eater, or herbivore. Hawks and snakes are second-level consumers. They are carnivores, or meat eaters, because they eat other animals. Animals that eat plants and animals are omnivores, meaning they "eat all." Humans are omnivores.

Cycles in Nature

Many things interact in ecosystems. Plants take a gas called carbon dioxide from the air. They release oxygen. Animals take oxygen from the air. They release carbon dioxide. In this cycle, plants and animals benefit each other.

Energy Pyramid

All living things use, lose, and store energy. An energy pyramid shows how energy moves through an ecosystem. Producers make up the base of the pyramid. Next are first-level consumers. Second-level and third-level consumers are in the upper levels.

An energy pyramid helps explain populations in ecosystems. Producers usually have the largest populations because they have the most energy to use. Their energy comes straight from the sun. Energy is released every time food is digested and the energy is used to move around. Much of this energy is lost to the surrounding environment as heat. As a result, there is less energy available at each level of the pyramid. After three or four links between consumers, there is just not as much energy for an animal to use. Therefore, there are only a few third-level consumers.

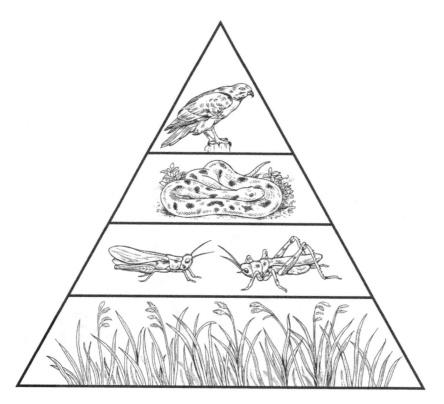

Life Science
Core Skills Science, Grade 5

Name _____ Date _____

What Is a Food Web?

Fill in the blanks.

1. A producer makes its own food from raw materials and energy from

   _____.

2. A consumer gets energy by _____ food,
   not producing it.

3. Write the name of a plant or animal on each part of the diagram to show a food chain.

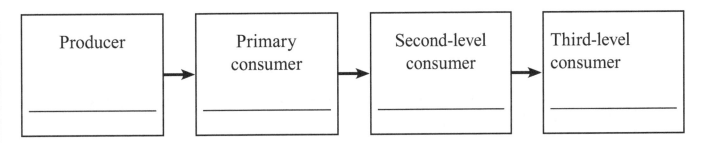

Producer	Primary consumer	Second-level consumer	Third-level consumer
_____	_____	_____	_____

4. Bacteria, fungi, and earthworms are all _____.

5. A rabbit is a(n) _____, meaning "plant eater."

6. Hawks and snakes are _____, which means "meat eaters."

7. Animals that eat both plants and animals are called _____.

8. Animals release carbon dioxide and take in _____.

9. As a general rule, _____ have the largest populations
   because they have the most energy available to them.

10. **Main Idea** Describe how energy flows through an ecosystem.

   _____

   _____

Life Science
Core Skills Science, Grade 5

11. Vocabulary Compare a food chain with a food web. Use both terms to explain how animals interact with and depend on one another.

_____

_____

_____

12. Reading Skill: Classify Give one example each of a producer, herbivore, carnivore, omnivore, and decomposer.

_____

_____

_____

13. Critical Thinking: Apply What would happen to an ecosystem if a drought killed half of the plants that lived there?

_____

_____

_____

14. Inquiry Skill: Use Models List the things you ate for breakfast today. Use the list to construct one or more food chains for each food.

_____

15. Test Prep Unlike a carnivore, a herbivore

    A makes its own food.

    B eats only producers.

    C eats other animals.

    D eats both plants and animals.

What Are Habitats and Niches?

Habitats

Telling people your street address is a simple way to describe where your house is. All living things have an "address." A habitat is the area where an organism lives. Everything that an organism needs to live can be found in its habitat. Many different living things may share a habitat.

Niches

Organisms in a habitat have specific tasks. A niche is what an organism does in its habitat. A niche includes where the organism lives, how it reproduces, and how it stays safe. For example, on the savanna, the niche of a lion includes hunting zebra. The niche of a zebra includes eating grass.

Each group of organisms in a habitat uses resources in a different way. In the savanna, for example, zebras eat the grass. Lions do not eat the grass, but they lie on the grass. Birds use the grass to build nests. Using resources differently means there are enough resources for everyone.

Adaptations

An adaptation is something that helps an organism survive in its environment. Some adaptations are physical. The sea turtle has flippers that help it move through water. The desert turtle has feet that help it move easily across the sand. Each animal's body has special parts to help it live in its habitat.

Other adaptations are things an organism does. A bat might adapt by sleeping through winter. This adaptation, called hibernation, allows bats to live in cold places.

Natural Selection

In the 1880s, a scientist named Charles Darwin suggested a way to explain adaptations. He said that some members of a species have features that help them live in their environment. The members with special features are more likely to survive. Then their babies inherit those features.

33

This process is known as natural selection. For example, birds of a certain species live on a beach and search for food among the rocks. Some of the birds have long, pointed beaks. They can easily pick up food from the cracks between the rocks. Other birds in the population have shorter, rounder beaks and cannot reach the food as well.

The birds with pointed beaks are more likely to stay alive when food becomes scarce. Their babies will also have pointed beaks. After several generations, almost all birds of this species will have the longer, more pointed beaks.

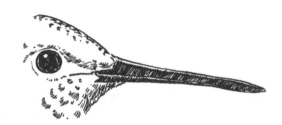

Symbiosis

All living things depend on and affect one another. Some organisms develop close relationships. Symbiosis is a close, long-lasting relationship between two different organisms.

There are three kinds of symbiosis. In parasitism, one organism in the relationship is helped and the other is hurt. In commensalism, one organism is helped and one is not affected. In mutualism, both organisms are helped.

Kinds of Symbiosis

Parasitism	Commensalism	Mutualism
This lamprey takes blood from its host. The lamprey is helped. Its host is hurt.	Owls live in this cactus. The owl is helped and the cactus is not affected.	Tiny shrimp can eat parasites on fish. The shrimp and the fish are helped.

Name _____ Date _____

What Are Habitats and Niches?

Write answers to the questions on the lines below.

1. What is a habitat?

_____

_____

2. What is a niche?

_____

_____

_____

_____

_____

_____

3. Write at least one adaptation for each animal shown above.

4. What is symbiosis?

_____

_____

5. What is parasitism?

_____

_____

6. Main Idea Describe two different niches in a savanna habitat.

_____

_____

7. Vocabulary What is mutualism? Describe how mutualism affects organisms.

_____

_____

8. Reading Skill: Compare and Contrast According to natural selection, how do differences among organisms help develop adaptations?

_____

_____

_____

9. Critical Thinking: Apply How would you describe your niche in the environment? How does it compare to an animal's niche in nature?

_____

_____

_____

10. Inquiry Skill: Observe Describe a type of symbiotic relationship that you have observed. Identify which organisms benefit and which are harmed, if any.

_____

_____

11. Test Prep An organism's niche includes

    A where it lives.

    B how it protects itself.

    C how it reproduces.

    D all of the above.

What Are the Layers That Make Up Earth?

Earth's Major Systems

Earth can be divided into four main parts, or spheres. First, there is the geosphere, which includes the solid and molten rock, soil, and sediments that make up all of the land on Earth. Next, there is the atmosphere, which contains all the air on the planet. The third sphere is the hydrosphere, which comprises all Earth's water. It includes oceans, rivers, and even ice. Finally, there is the biosphere, which consists of all living things. Each of these spheres is a complex system with many parts.

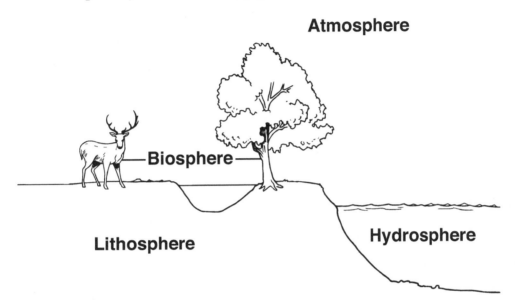

The Geosphere

The geosphere includes everything from the layers of minerals and rock beneath Earth's surface to the landforms that we see every day. Most of the geosphere is found beneath our feet. Earth has three layers that stretch from the soil to the very center of the planet. Those layers are the crust, mantle, and core. The geosphere is also made up of rocks on the surface. Mountains, volcanoes, canyons, cliffs, and hills are all part of this sphere.

The Atmosphere

Many gases surround Earth. They include nitrogen, oxygen, and carbon dioxide, among others. Together, these gases are known as the atmosphere. Gases in the atmosphere can be added and taken away. For example, when people and animals breathe, they take in oxygen. They also let out carbon dioxide.

The atmosphere is made up of four layers, each of which is a different temperature. The layer closest to Earth's surface is where weather occurs. The atmosphere also controls heat on Earth.

Earth Science
Core Skills Science, Grade 5

The Hydrosphere

Streams, glaciers, and lakes all contain water and are therefore all part of the hydrosphere. The hydrosphere's water can be in solid or liquid form. Oceans are where most of Earth's available water is located. However, water can also be found in less obvious places, like under the ground and in the atmosphere. Most of the fresh water on Earth is actually located underground or in glaciers. The remaining water not in oceans or in these locations can be found in streams, lakes, wetlands, and the atmosphere. But that water only makes up a tiny fraction of the total water in Earth's hydrosphere.

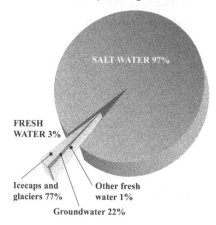

Distribution of Water in the Hydrosphere

The Biosphere

All of Earth's living things, including plants, animals, human beings, and bacteria, are part of the biosphere. The biosphere overlaps with the other three spheres. Living things can be found in the air, water, and ground.

The biosphere is a closed system. Energy comes in and out, but matter does not. Plants get their energy from the sun and use it to make food. The energy is transferred to animals when they eat the plants. Some of the energy is lost to the environment as heat. But plants and animals never leave the system. They are broken down and absorbed by the environment when they die.

How Earth's Systems Interact

Earth's four systems regularly interact and work together to affect the many materials and processes on this planet. For example, the ocean is home to many plants and animals. And the atmosphere keeps Earth at the temperatures necessary to keep living things in the biosphere alive.

The water in oceans affects the atmosphere. The sun sometimes causes ocean water to heat up. This happens because the ocean absorbs the sun's energy. The heat from the ocean affects temperature and climate in the atmosphere. It often causes storms, which carry rain from the hydrosphere. When storms occur, they affect the geosphere. Rain often causes landforms to wear away in a process called erosion. Erosion is also caused by wind in the atmosphere.

38

Name _____ Date _____

What Are the Layers That Make Up Earth?

Write answers to the questions on the lines below.

1. What are three things found in the geosphere?

   _____

2. What gases are found in the atmosphere?

   _____

3. Where can most of Earth's fresh water be found?

   _____

4. What makes the biosphere a closed system?

   _____

5. What is one way that the biosphere and hydrosphere interact?

   _____

   _____

6. How do oceans in the hydrosphere affect the atmosphere?

   _____

   _____

7. Which spheres are involved in the process of erosion?

   _____

8. Main Idea Give a brief description of each of Earth's spheres.

_____

_____

9. Vocabulary Explain the multiple meanings of the word *sphere*.

_____

_____

10. Reading Skill: Summarize Summarize how water is distributed on Earth.

_____

_____

11. Critical Thinking: Apply How might a thunderstorm affect the biosphere and geosphere?

_____

_____

12. Inquiry Skill: Observe Go to a park or other outdoor environment and observe nature for an hour. Look for and record examples of each of Earth's spheres. Note any interactions between the four spheres that you observe.

_____

_____

_____

13. Test Prep Bacteria is part of the

    A geosphere.

    B hydrosphere.

    C atmosphere.

    D biosphere.

What Makes Up Earth's Surface?

The features, or parts, of Earth's surface include solid landforms and water. You can identify Earth's surface features by their location, shape, and elevation.

Earth's Solid Surface

Earth's rocky outer layer is called the crust. On the surface of the crust are huge masses of land called continents. Features found on the continents are often called landforms. Features of the crust are also found on the ocean floor.

Mountains are Earth's tallest landforms. Their steep slopes rise to tall peaks. Hills with rounded tops are smaller than mountains. Mountain valleys are long, narrow areas of low land between mountains or hills. Deep valleys with steep sides are called canyons.

Plateaus are high landforms with mostly flat surfaces. Plains are broad and flat. There are wide plains in the middle of the United States.

A river valley has a river flowing through it. The river usually flows through the center of the valley. A flood plain is the floor of a river valley on either side of the river. Water covers a flood plain when a river rises above its banks.

A Watery Planet

Most of Earth's water is found in oceans, which are huge bodies of salt water. All of Earth's oceans are connected. They form one great world ocean. Salt water covers 68% of Earth's surface. In contrast, land covers 29% of Earth's surface.

Some of Earth's water is on the continents in lakes, rivers, streams, and ponds. It is called fresh water because it is not salty. Only 3% of Earth's water is fresh water. It is a valuable resource because things that live on land need fresh water to survive.

Coastal Features

Different landforms are found near water. A coastal plain is a wide flat area near an ocean. Where dry land meets the ocean is called the shore.

41

Ocean Floor Features

A feature called the continental margin starts at the water's edge. The continental margin is made up of the continental shelf, the continental slope, and the continental rise.

The continental shelf forms the edges of continents. Farther from the shelf is the continental slope. The continental slope drops sharply. It forms the sides of continents.
At the bottom of the slope is the continental rise. It stretches out across the ocean floor.

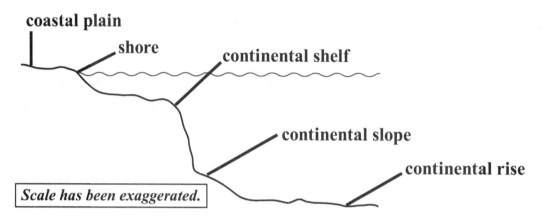

coastal plain

shore

continental shelf

continental slope

continental rise

Scale has been exaggerated.

Mid-Ocean Features

Far from the continental margin, the ocean basin contains many features. Here, deep canyons called trenches cut into the ocean floor. Underwater mountains are numerous. Some mountain peaks stick out of the water as islands.

Mapping Surface Features

A topographic map shows the shape of surface features and their elevations. Elevation is the height of a landform above sea level. Contour lines connect points on the map that have the same elevation. Contour lines can show the shape and steepness of the land.

This topographic map shows Mount Rainier in Washington State. The numbers on the contour lines show elevation in feet.

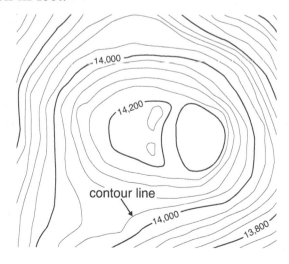

14,000

14,200

contour line

14,000

13,800

42

Name _____ Date _____

What Makes Up Earth's Surface?

The graph represents the area of Earth's surface. Fill in the blanks in the graph using the terms *salt water*, *land*, and *fresh water*.

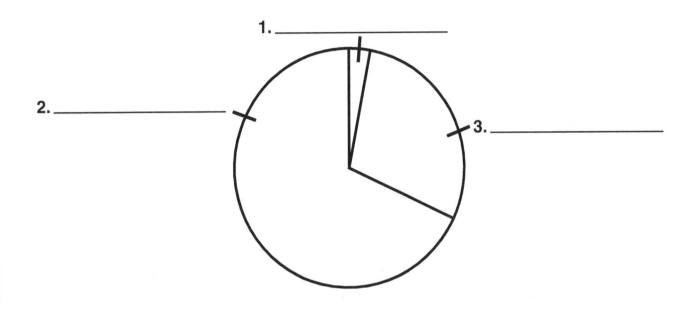

1. _____

2. _____

3. _____

Fill in the blanks.

4. _____ are long, narrow regions of low land between ranges of mountains or hills.

5. In the middle of the United States, there are _____.

6. _____ and _____ are two features of the ocean basin.

7. The _____ is the region beyond the continental margin.

8. **Main Idea** What three properties are used to identify surface features?

_____

_____

9. **Vocabulary** How do contour lines help you visualize a feature of Earth's solid surface?

_____

_____

10. **Reading Skill: Main Idea and Details** Name and describe the three parts of the continental margin.

_____

_____

_____

11. **Critical Thinking: Analyze** Earth has lots of water. Water covers more than 70% of Earth's surface. Even so, water is a critical resource for all living things. Explain why.

_____

_____

12. **Inquiry Skill: Compare** Describe how plateaus and plains are similar and how they are different.

_____

_____

13. **Test Prep** Trenches are a feature of the ocean floor. What land feature does their shape most resemble?

   A river valley

   B canyon

   C mountain range

   D beach

How Is Earth's Surface Worn Down and Built Up?

Weathering

Earth's crust is made mostly of rock. The rocks are broken into pieces by weathering. Weathering is a destructive force. Destructive forces break things down. There are two types of weathering: mechanical and chemical.

Mechanical weathering is the breaking of larger rocks into smaller pieces. These smaller pieces of rock are called sediment. Ice causes much mechanical weathering. Water gets into the cracks of rocks and freezes. When water turns to ice, it expands, or takes up more room. When this happens, rocks break apart.

Moving air and water also cause mechanical weathering. Blown sand or rushing water hits rocks, and the rocks get weaker. Over time, they crack or crumble. Mechanical weathering breaks rocks, but it does not change the kind of rocks they are. In chemical weathering, rocks change into other materials.

Water causes most chemical weathering. Water can dissolve some rocks, or break them down into parts that become part of the water. Water trickling through the ground can dissolve some rocks far under the surface. Caves are hollow spaces under the ground that are formed by weathering. Most caves are made from limestone. Weak acid dissolves limestone easily. Water seeps into the ground and dissolves some rock. Over time, holes form in the rock. The holes grow, forming passages, chambers, and pits. Slowly, they become caves.

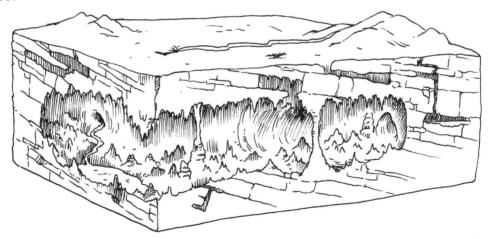

Erosion

Erosion occurs when sediments are carried away by wind, water, or ice. Flowing water in streams and rivers wears away the ground. This erosion can carve a valley or canyon.

Glaciers are huge sheets of ice that wear down and shape Earth's surface features. Thousands of years ago glaciers helped shape the plains of what is now the United States and carved out the Great Lakes.

45

Ocean waves also wear down Earth's surface. Crashing waves break down rock along coastlines. Waves drag sediment back and forth, which creates sand.

Slow and Fast Changes

Erosion keeps changing the landscape. In general, destructive forces act very slowly. However, sometimes such changes happen much faster.

Caves can take thousands of years to form. However, after a cave has formed, the rock above the cave often has little support. At some point, the rock above the cave may sink or fall into the hole made by the cave. This is called a sinkhole. Sinkholes can form very suddenly. One large sinkhole formed in a single day in Winter Park, Florida. The city sealed it and made a lake.

Landslides also happen suddenly. Erosion is one cause of landslides. Landslides are large masses of earth and rocks that tumble down a steep slope. Several destructive forces help cause landslides. Erosion from rivers, rain, glaciers, or ocean water may make a slope steeper. It may also make sediments looser. If the sediments get soaked with water, they may slide. Any movement of Earth, such as an earthquake, can form cracks or shake rocks loose. This movement can start landslides.

Deposition

Deposition and other forces build up Earth's surface features. Deposition occurs when sediments are moved from one place to another. For example, ocean waves drop sand on a beach. Flowing river water usually empties into a lake or ocean. The water slows down and drops sediment over the land at the end of the river.

Pushing Up Earth's Surface

Magma is melted rock below Earth's surface. Pressure below the surface can cause magma to push up on Earth's crust. This pushing forms round, dome-shaped mountains.

Magma at Earth's surface is called lava. A large deposit of lava with sloping sides is called a shield cone. The Hawaiian Islands are the tops of several giant shield cones.

Surface features are also created when huge pieces of Earth's crust crash into each other. When this happens, the crust rises to form high mountains. The Himalaya Mountains began forming this way about 65 million years ago.

Coral reefs are an ocean feature made from tiny animals called corals. As corals die, their skeletons build up into a bumpy ridge called a reef. Some reefs are built around islands.

46

How Is Earth's Surface Worn Down and Built Up?

Fill in the blanks.

1. Mechanical weathering is the breaking of larger rocks into smaller pieces of rock, called _____.

2. _____ is the carrying away of sediments by moving water, wind, or moving ice.

3. _____ are huge sheets of ice that wear down Earth's surface features.

4. When the rock above a cave collapses, it forms a(n) _____.

5. Large masses of earth and rocks that tumble down a steep slope are called

_____.

Write answers to the questions on the lines below.

6. What is deposition?

_____

_____

7. What is a shield cone?

_____

_____

8. How did the Himalaya Mountains form?

_____

_____

9. How are coral reefs formed?

_____

_____

10. Main Idea Why are weathering and erosion considered destructive forces?

_____

_____

11. Vocabulary Why is deposition described as the opposite of erosion? Give examples of these processes.

_____

_____

12. Reading Skill: Cause and Effect Describe the sequence of events in the formation of sand.

_____

_____

_____

13. Critical Thinking: Synthesize The Hawaiian Islands are the tops of shield cones. What can you conclude about where shield cones form?

_____

_____

_____

14. Inquiry Skill: Infer What can the size and shape of a sand dune tell you about how it was formed?

_____

_____

_____

15. Test Prep When a river meets an ocean, sediments drop out of the river because the river

    A speeds up.

    B slows down.

    C becomes saltier.

    D flows uphill.

What Is Earth's Structure?

Hot Inside

Geysers are boiling fountains of water that shoot up from Earth's surface. Hot rocks under the surface heat water. Pressure forces the water up. The existence of geysers tells us that Earth is very hot inside. People study geysers and volcanoes to learn about temperatures inside Earth.

Earth's Layers

Each of Earth's layers has a different thickness. The outer layer, or crust, is much thinner than the other layers. The crust is mostly solid rock. The layer just below Earth's crust is the mantle. It is the thickest layer, and is composed of flowing rock material. The solid upper part of the mantle joins with the crust to form the lithosphere. At the center of Earth is the core. The outer core is the only layer that is all liquid. The inner core is even hotter. Both core layers contain very hot iron and nickel.

Earthquakes

An earthquake is a violent shaking of Earth's crust caused by the sudden release of built-up energy. This release of energy usually occurs when rocks move along a fault. A fault is a crack, or break, in Earth's crust between two blocks of rock. The rocks on either side of a fault usually remain still. But when stress builds up, they can bend and fold. The rocks slide against each other and an earthquake occurs.

As the rocks slide into new positions, seismic waves, or vibrations, travel through the Earth in all directions. The epicenter, right above the fault, is where the earthquake is most intense. Seismic waves here are the strongest. It is seismic waves that have allowed scientists to learn more about how earthquakes and Earth's interior work. Scientists use this knowledge to try to predict when and where earthquakes will occur. They still do not have a perfect method of doing this, but scientists continue to test different solutions.

Earthquakes occur when the rocks along a fault slide against each other.

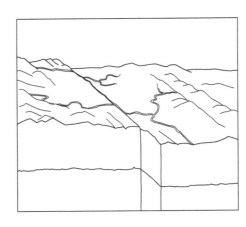

One method that scientists use for predicting earthquakes is to look for patterns. Both earthquakes and volcanoes tend to occur along boundaries between continents and oceans. The rocks along these boundaries usually experience greater stress. They collide, pull away from each other, or scrape against each other. Mountain ranges and ocean trenches tend to occur in these locations as well. Many earthquakes and volcanoes occur in an area called the Ring of Fire. It borders the Pacific Ocean.

Volcanoes

A volcano is an opening in Earth's surface through which melted rock, hot gases, rock pieces, and ash erupt. Most volcanoes start below the surface where it is so hot that rock melts. This melted rock is called magma.

When rock melts, it lets out gases. The gas makes the magma lighter than the solid rock around it. Slowly, the gas-filled magma rises. It is under great pressure from the weight of surrounding rock. Once near the surface, the gas and magma burst through a central opening, or vent. The rock ash and other material build up, forming a volcano.

Three main kinds of material come out of volcanoes during an eruption. Most of the material is lava. Lava is the name for magma after it reaches the surface. Rock pieces may form when gas in sticky magma cannot escape. Pressure builds up until the gas blasts the magma apart. The pieces erupt into dust, ash, and large chunks called bombs. Gases also escape when a volcano erupts. Gases from volcanoes are mostly steam. They often have harmful chemicals in them. These gases mix with ash to form a deadly black smoke.

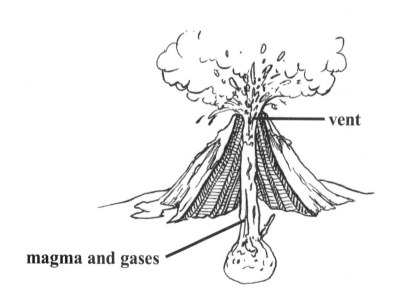

vent

magma and gases

Name _____ Date _____

What Is Earth's Structure?

Write answers to the questions on the lines below.

1. What information does the existence of geysers and volcanoes provide scientists about Earth's interior?

   _____

   _____

2. Beginning at the surface and moving inward, list the four main layers that make up Earth's structure.

   _____

   _____

3. What are faults?

   _____

   _____

4. Why is the intensity of an earthquake strongest at the epicenter?

   _____

   _____

5. What are seismic waves?

   _____

6. What is magma?

   _____

7. What causes a volcano to erupt?

   _____

8. What are three materials that come from a volcano when it erupts?

   _____

Earth Science
Core Skills Science, Grade 5

9. Main Idea Why do earthquakes and volcanoes usually occur along continent and ocean boundaries?

_____

_____

10. Vocabulary What parts of Earth's structure combine to form the lithosphere?

_____

_____

11. Reading Skill: Cause and Effect Describe the cause-and-effect relationship that creates geysers.

_____

_____

_____

12. Critical Thinking: Draw Conclusions How do you think the Ring of Fire got its name?

_____

_____

13. Inquiry Skill: Use Models Describe how you would use small rocks, pieces of board, and a tub of water to model Earth's lithosphere.

_____

_____

_____

14. Test Prep The thinnest layer of Earth's structure is the

    A crust.

    B lithosphere.

    C inner core.

    D mantle.

How Do People Use Resources and Soil?

Earth provides many resources, or useful things, that people need. Some resources are found only in small amounts. Other resources seem like they may never run out.

Natural Resources

The natural world gives us everything that we need to stay alive. These natural resources include air, water, minerals, and soil. People use natural resources to build houses and grow crops. We use natural resources as fuel. Natural resources used to make energy are called energy resources.

Nonrenewable Resources

Resources that are not easy to get back after they are gone are called nonrenewable resources. Nonrenewable resources include oil, natural gas, and coal. These resources are called fossil fuels. They are called fossil fuels because they come from the remains, or parts, of plants and animals that died long ago.

Renewable Resources

Resources that are easy to make more of or that can be reused are renewable resources. Farm crops, animals, oxygen, fresh water, and trees are renewable resources.

Renewable resources used to make energy are called alternative energy sources. We can use them instead of fossil fuels. Sun, wind, and water are alternative energy sources.

Energy from the sun is called solar energy. Two machines that can collect sunlight and change it into energy are solar panels and solar cells. Solar panels change sunlight into heat energy. Solar cells change sunlight into electricity.

Windmills have been used for hundreds of years to move water and to grind grain. Today, wind farms use rows of wind turbines to power machines that make electricity. Wind turbines are like old-fashioned windmills. They have blades that turn as the wind blows. The energy from the moving blades is changed into electricity.

Electrical power that is made from moving water is called hydroelectric power. Hydroelectric power is made by holding water behind a dam and slowly letting it out. The water turns turbines and the energy is changed to electricity.

Conservation

The careful use of resources is called conservation. Conserving nonrenewable resources like fossil fuels helps save them for the future.

Conserving fossil fuels cuts down on pollution. Pollution is anything that dirties our air, soil, and water. Smoke from burning fossil fuels can mix with water to form smog. Smog is not healthy to breathe.

Other waste gases from fossil fuels mix with water in the air to form acid rain, another kind of pollution. Acid rain can kill trees and fish and can harm buildings.

What Is Soil?

Soil is made up of minerals, small rocks, water, and humus, or the decaying remains of living things. Humus adds nutrients to the soil. The type of soil depends on the weather and living matter in a particular place.

Soil begins with weathering, the breaking down of rock into smaller pieces. Below soil, rock that has not been weathered is bedrock. Bedrock eventually begins to break down and become part of the soil. This soil is called residual soil.

Over time, layers of soil form soil horizons. A fully formed soil has four horizons. Together, all soil horizons form a soil profile. From the top down, the horizons are topsoil, subsoil, parent material, and bedrock. Horizons also have letter names.

Horizon A is topsoil. This soil has humus, minerals, and bits of rock, as well as insects and earthworms. It is the richest soil, and most plant seeds begin to grow here. Horizon B is subsoil, which has very little humus. Water washes down some nutrients and decaying remains from the topsoil. Some plant roots can reach into this soil, and some living things may be found here. Horizon C is chunks of weathered bedrock called parent material. It is called parent material because soil comes from it. Horizon D is bedrock, upon which the upper layers of soil rest.

Farmers protect topsoil by planting a windbreak. This is a line of trees along the edge of a field. A windbreak blocks the wind so it cannot blow away the topsoil.

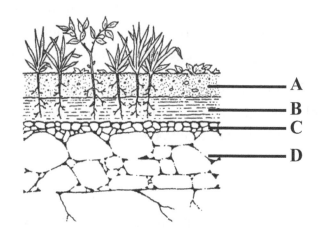

Name _____ Date _____

How Do People Use Resources and Soil?

Fill in the blanks.

1. Things from the natural world that people need to live or find useful are called

   _____.

2. Oil, natural gas, and coal are examples of _____ fuels.

3. Hydroelectric power plants use _____ to
   generate electricity.

4. _____ are resources that cannot be easily replaced.

5. Trees, sun, water, and wind are examples of _____
   resources.

6. Soil that forms from the bedrock beneath is called _____.

7. Humus adds _____ to soil.

8. Over time, as soil develops, definite layers called

   _____ can be observed.

9. Most plant seeds germinate, or sprout, in _____.

10. A _____ is a line of trees planted along the edge of
    a field to help block the wind and prevent or reduce soil erosion.

Earth Science
Core Skills Science, Grade 5

11. Main Idea Why is solar energy called a renewable resource?

_____

_____

12. Vocabulary In your own words, define the term *soil profile*.

_____

_____

13. Reading Skill: Problem and Solution Which alternative energy resource do you think is most likely to replace fossil fuels in the future?

_____

_____

_____

14. Critical Thinking: Evaluate Where are the best places to build wind farms? Explain your reasoning.

_____

_____

_____

15. Inquiry Skill: Observe You dig up part of your yard in hope of planting a garden. You see that the uppermost layer of soil is thin, and you find a lot of rocks near the surface. What does this tell you about how your garden will grow?

_____

_____

_____

16. Test Prep The layer of mature soil that contains only a few nutrients is the

   A bedrock.

   B parent material.

   C subsoil.

   D topsoil.

What Factors Affect Climate?

Climate is the normal pattern of weather in an area over many years. The climate is affected by Earth's shape, the way Earth is tilted, and Earth's land and water. Uneven heating of Earth's surface by the sun creates three major climate zones.

Uneven Heating

Some places on Earth are warmer than others. That is because the sun does not heat all places evenly.

The sun's rays hit different parts of Earth at different angles. The sun's rays hit places near the equator at a 90-degree angle. These places are warm all year long. In other places, such as the poles, the sun's rays hit at less than a 90-degree angle. These places are usually cooler.

Major Climate Zones

There are three major climate zones. Each one has different temperatures and amounts of precipitation, or any kind of water that falls from clouds. Rain, snow, sleet, and hail are types of precipitation.

Tropical climates are near the equator. They are very warm. Although some tropical climates are dry, usually it rains often. Temperate climates are found north and south of tropical climates. Some temperate climates have mild summers and winters. Some have warm summers and cold winters. Polar climates are near the North and South Poles. They are always cold and snowy.

tropical climate

temperate climate

polar climate

Land and Sea Breezes

Shorelines are windy places. The land and sea are not heated evenly. The unequal heating causes sea breezes and land breezes.

Sea breezes occur during the day. The land heats up faster than the water. Warm air over land rises, and cool air over the water moves in to take its place. Sea breezes blow from sea to land.

Land breezes occur at night. Land cools faster than water, so air over the water is warmer. The cool air over the land moves toward the sea. Land breezes blow from land to sea.

Mountain Effect

Mountains near oceans affect the water cycle and help create rainy climates. First, water evaporates from the ocean and becomes water vapor in the air. The warm, moist air rises and moves toward land. The air meets the mountain and cools as it is forced up. When the air cools to below the dew-point temperature, there is more condensation than evaporation and a cloud forms.

Next, the clouds drop rain on the windward side of the mountain. That side, where wind hits the mountain, is near the ocean. Then the clouds pass to the other side of the mountain, the leeward side. There is not much water vapor left in the clouds, so little rain falls on this side.

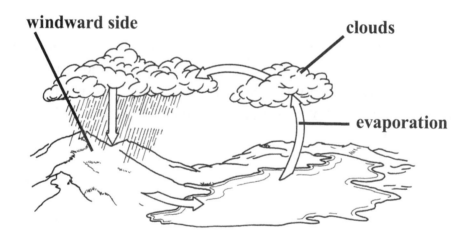

Oceans and Climate

Places near the equator absorb more energy from the sun than places near the poles. Ocean waters are warmest at the equator and coldest near the poles.

Winds blowing across the ocean create moving streams of water called ocean currents. Warm currents move warm water toward the poles. Cold currents move cold water toward the equator. These currents make climates warmer or cooler.

Sometimes ocean currents change. Every five to seven years, El Niño events cause warm ocean currents in the Pacific Ocean to change direction. This shift can change the climates.

58

Name _____ Date _____

What Factors Affect Climate?

Fill in the chart. Write one fact about each climate zone.

Polar	Temperate	Tropical
1. _____ _____ _____	2. _____ _____ _____	3. _____ _____ _____

Fill in the blanks.

4. The sun provides the energy for liquid water to become

   _____ in the air.

5. Mountains near oceans affect the _____, the movement of water between Earth's atmosphere and land.

6. Rain and snow fall mostly on the _____ side of mountains.

7. The drier side of a mountain is the _____.

8. Regions near the _____ absorb more energy from the sun than those near the poles.

9. _____ events occur every five to seven years and can cause temporary changes in climate around the globe.

10. **Main Idea** What are some factors that affect climate?

   _____

   _____

11. Vocabulary What are ocean currents? What sets them in motion?

_____

_____

_____

12. Reading Skill: Cause and Effect Describe two ways in which bodies of water can affect climate. Use these words in your answer: *land breeze, sea breeze,* and *ocean current*.

_____

_____

_____

13. Critical Thinking: Synthesize Why is the climate hot at places along the equator?

_____

_____

_____

14. Inquiry Skill: Communicate Write a paragraph detailing the characteristics of tropical, temperate, and polar climates.

_____

_____

_____

15. Test Prep Ocean currents affect climate because they

    A are always cold.

    B are always warm.

    C move water and energy from one place to another.

    D cause winds to move air from one place to another.

How Are Weather Forecasts Made?

Gases surrounding the Earth are called the atmosphere. When the atmosphere changes, weather changes. People use different tools to learn what the weather will be like.

Composition of Earth's Atmosphere

Earth's atmosphere is a mixture of gases that surrounds the planet like a blanket. It is mostly made up of two gases, nitrogen and oxygen. Carbon dioxide is a gas that is also in the atmosphere. When fossil fuels are burned on Earth, the amount of carbon dioxide goes up.

Structure of the Atmosphere

Earth's atmosphere has four layers. Each layer has a different temperature. The farther away a layer is from Earth, the colder it is. These layers cause air pressure, which affects Earth's weather.

The troposphere is the layer closest to Earth. This is where almost all weather takes place. It is the thinnest layer, but most of the gases in the atmosphere are in it. The next layer up is the stratosphere. It helps protect life on Earth from the sun's radiation. The third layer, the mesosphere, is the coldest part of the atmosphere. The fourth layer, the thermosphere, is the first part of the atmosphere that sunlight hits.

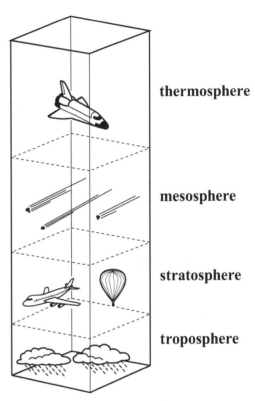

Air Masses

An air mass is a body of air that has roughly the same temperature and moisture throughout. Some air masses are warm, while others are cold. Air masses also have different amounts of moisture. Some are dry, while others are moist. The amount of moisture depends on where the air mass is formed.

Continental air masses form over land and are dry. They usually bring fair weather. Maritime air masses form over water and are moist. They often bring fog and rain to coastal areas. They also bring moisture to the middle of the country.

Fronts

When two air masses meet, a front forms. A weather front is the boundary between two air masses that have different properties. For example, one air mass may be cool, and the other may be warm. Most fronts change the weather.

Warm fronts often bring clouds and light rain. A warm front is shown with a red line on a weather map. Cold fronts often bring heavy rain or thunderstorms. A cold front is shown with a blue line on a weather map. Sometimes two air masses meet, but neither one moves forward. This is called a stationary front.

Stationary Front

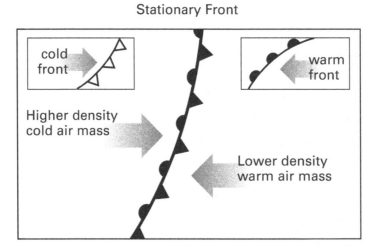

Observing Weather

Meteorologists are scientists who study weather. They record observations about weather on weather maps. When they study the map, they can tell what the future weather might be like. Weather maps show temperatures, precipitation, and areas of high and low pressure.

Radar can be used to observe weather. It can help predict weather. Radar makes an image of a storm. It can show the size of a storm and any rain or snow. It can also show how fast a storm is moving and in what direction. Having this information can help people prepare for dangerous weather.

Satellites are also used to learn about weather. These machines orbit high above Earth. They gather information about the atmosphere and send it back to meteorologists. Satellites can also be used to study clouds and storms.

Other tools are used to measure weather. Thermometers measure temperature. Rain gauges measure the amount of rain or snow. Anemometers measure wind speed. Barometers measure air pressure. Weather vanes show which way the wind is blowing.

How Are Weather Forecasts Made?

Fill in the blanks.

1. Earth's atmosphere is made up mostly of _____.

2. The _____ is where almost all weather takes place.

3. The _____ protects life on Earth from the sun.

4. _____ air masses form over water and are moist.

5. When _____ air masses move into an area, they generally bring fair weather.

6. A warm front generally brings _____.

7. _____ can be used to create an image of a storm.

8. _____ orbit high above Earth and use instruments to gather data from the upper atmosphere.

9. **Main Idea** What are the four main layers of Earth's atmosphere?

_____

_____

Earth Science
Core Skills Science, Grade 5

10. Vocabulary What is an air mass and what determines its properties?

_____

_____

11. Reading Skill: Draw Conclusions Suppose your area is experiencing thunderstorms. What kinds of changes in the atmosphere led to the formation of the storms?

_____

_____

_____

12. Critical Thinking: Apply How might radar images help to reduce damage from an approaching storm?

_____

_____

_____

13. Inquiry Skill: Collaborate How might sharing data gathered in different regions allow scientists to better predict the weather?

_____

_____

_____

14. Test Prep Weather fronts form when

    A air masses meet.

    B air masses form.

    C cold air rises.

    D warm air sinks.

What Are Stars and Galaxies?

What Are Stars and Galaxies?

A star is a huge ball of very hot gases. It gives off light, heat, and other kinds of energy. Stars can be grouped by their size, color, brightness, and temperature, and they can shine for billions of years.

The sun is a star that is medium in size and brightness. Many other stars are larger and brighter. Why does the sun look so much brighter than any other star? The reason is that the sun is much closer to Earth than any other star. Light from the sun takes about eight minutes to reach Earth. In comparison, light from the next closest star takes over four years to reach Earth. The sun's energy has been giving Earth light and heat for 4.5 billion years.

Constellations

A constellation is a group of stars that forms a pattern in the night sky. One well-known constellation is called Ursa Major, which means "Great Bear." Some of the stars in Ursa Major make up another group of stars called the Big Dipper. There are many other constellations as well, including one that looks like a lion and another that looks like a hunter. The sky is full of constellations.

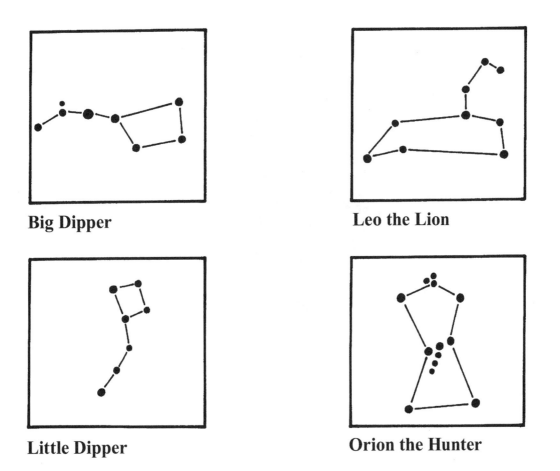

Big Dipper

Leo the Lion

Little Dipper

Orion the Hunter

Earth Science
Core Skills Science, Grade 5

Have you ever looked at a bright star early in the evening? If you look for it again later that night, it will seem to be in a different spot. The stars do not actually move, however; it is the rotation of the Earth that causes their apparent movement. As Earth rotates on its axis, you see different parts of the sky. As a result, the stars look like they are moving across the sky at night. There are stars in the sky during the day as well, but the brightness of the sun makes it impossible for you to see them.

Galaxies

The sun, the planets, and the moons are part of the solar system. The solar system is part of a larger group, too. It is part of a galaxy, which is a huge system, or group, of stars held together by gravity.

The solar system is in a spiral-shaped galaxy called the Milky Way. The stars and planets that you see at night are in the Milky Way. Not all galaxies are spiral shaped, however. Some are oval or round, and others are irregular.

The universe is made up of all the matter and energy there is, including all the galaxies and their stars, planets, and moons. There are billions of galaxies in the universe, and no one knows how big the universe truly is. Scientists have discovered that it continues to grow larger and larger.

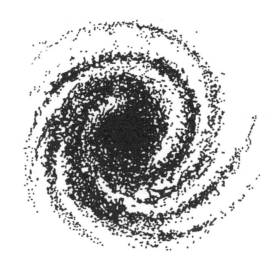

Name _____ Date _____

What Are Stars and Galaxies?

Fill in the blanks.

1. Four ways that stars can be classified are _____

   _____.

2. The sun appears brighter and larger than other stars because it

   _____.

3. The sun is a star that is medium both in its _____ and its

   _____.

4. The Big Dipper is a _____.

5. Stars appear to move because _____.

6. The brightness of the sun makes it impossible to _____

   _____.

7. A galaxy is _____

   _____.

8. The Milky Way is _____

   _____.

9. There are billions of galaxies in the _____.

10. Main Idea What objects can be found in a galaxy?

_____

_____

_____

11. Vocabulary Write a sentence about the universe. Be sure to use the terms *galaxy* and *stars*.

_____

_____

12. Critical Thinking: Analyze Suppose the Sun were bigger and brighter. What would happen to Earth?

_____

13. Inquiry Skill: Observe Choose a picture from this lesson. Study the picture and write a detailed description of what you see.

_____

_____

_____

_____

14. Test Prep A constellation is a

    A young, growing star that is new to the universe.

    B ball of extremely hot gases that gives off energy.

    C group, or system, of stars held together by gravity.

    D group of stars that forms a pattern in the night sky.

What Causes Day and Night?

When students in the United States arrive home from school, it is already the next day in China. How is this possible? Planets revolve, or move in a path, around the sun. At the same time, planets rotate, or spin. Each planet spins around an axis, or an imaginary line that goes through the center of an object. Earth's axis goes through the North and South Poles.

Imagine the sunrise where you live. Although it appears that the sun is rising in the east, Earth is really just rotating on its axis. Your side of Earth is just beginning to face the sun, which signals that morning has begun. The side of Earth that faces the sun has daylight.

As the day goes on, the sun seems to move across the sky. In reality, however, Earth's rotating just makes it look that way. Earth continues to rotate throughout the day, and your side of Earth gradually turns away from the sun. As the sun appears to set in the west, your side is facing away from it. This signals the beginning of nighttime on your side of the world.

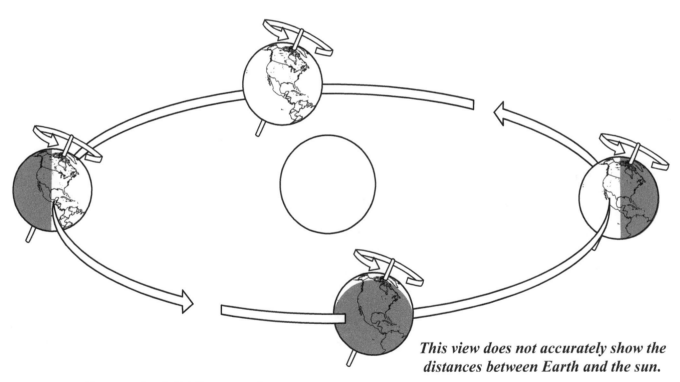

This view does not accurately show the distances between Earth and the sun.

Day and night happen because Earth rotates on its axis. As Earth spins, it revolves around the sun.

Earth Science
Core Skills Science, Grade 5

Days and nights do not always last the same amount of time. Their length is different on different parts of Earth, and it also changes during the year. The reason why this occurs is that some parts of Earth face the sun longer than other parts do.

Because Earth's axis tilts, the part of Earth tilted toward the sun gets more hours of light. Therefore, its day is longer. The part of Earth tilted away from the sun gets fewer hours of light, causing its night to be longer.

Earth continuously revolves around the sun. As Earth revolves, different parts are tilted toward the sun.

In June, the North Pole is tilted toward the sun. Places north of the equator face the sun for many hours each day. Because they do not face away from the sun for as long, they have more hours of daylight. This means that they also have fewer hours of darkness.

In December, the North Pole faces away from the sun. Places north of the equator face away from the sun for more hours than they face toward it, which results in more hours of darkness than daylight.

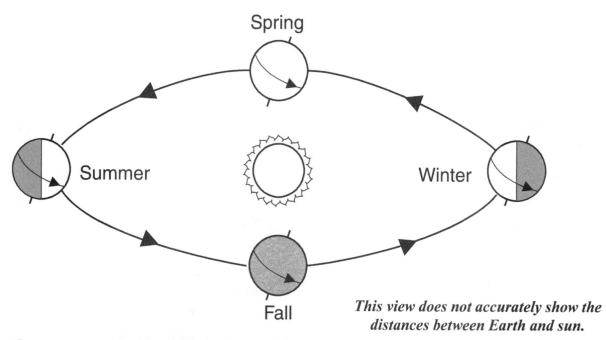

This view does not accurately show the distances between Earth and sun.

In summer, the North Pole faces toward the sun. In winter, the North Pole faces away from the sun.

Earth Science
Core Skills Science, Grade 5

Name _____ Date _____

What Causes Day and Night?

Write answers to the questions on the lines below.

1. Describe how Earth moves.

   _____

2. Describe planets' movements when they rotate.

   _____

3. What effect does Earth's rotation have on the planet's time of day?

   _____

   _____

4. Why does the length of day and night change throughout the year?

   _____

Use the diagram to answer the question below.

Washington, D.C.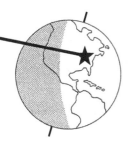

5. What are two things you can infer about Washington, D.C., based on Earth's position? Explain.

   _____

6. Main Idea Why does the sun appear to move across the sky?

_____

_____

7. Vocabulary If you spin a top that stays in one place, are you causing the top to rotate or revolve? Explain.

_____

_____

8. Reading Skill: Cause and Effect What is one effect of Earth's axis being tilted?

_____

9. Critical Thinking: Apply Sydney, Australia, is south of the equator. In January, the South Pole is tilted toward the sun. In Sydney, are there more hours of daylight or darkness in January? Explain.

_____

_____

10. Inquiry Skills: Use Models Describe how you could make a model of Earth revolving around the sun.

_____

_____

11. Test Prep How does Earth move?

   A It only revolves.

   B It only rotates.

   C It rotates and revolves.

   D It rotates in the morning and revolves at night.

What Causes Earth's Seasons?

You know that Earth rotates on its axis, causing day and night. Earth also revolves around the sun, causing the seasons.

Earth's Tilted Axis

Remember, Earth always rotates, or spins around, on its axis. The axis is like a line that goes from the North Pole through the center of Earth to the South Pole. This line is not straight up and down. It is tilted.

It takes 23 hours and 56 minutes for Earth to rotate once around. This time period is called a day. As Earth rotates, different parts face the sun. Remember, the side of Earth facing the sun has daytime. The side facing away from the sun has nighttime.

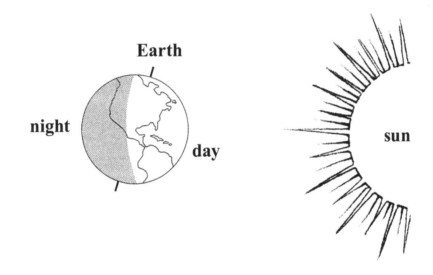

Earth also moves around the sun. One full trip around the sun is called a revolution, which takes a year, or $365\frac{1}{4}$ days.

Because Earth's axis is tilted, some parts of Earth are tilted toward the sun while other parts are tilted away. It is summer in the parts of Earth tilting toward the sun. It is winter in the parts of Earth tilting away from the sun.

Solstices and Equinoxes

On June 21 or 22 in the Northern Hemisphere, the North Pole points *toward* the sun. This is the summer solstice. It is the longest day of the year and marks the start of summer. At the same time, in the Southern Hemisphere it is winter because the South Pole is pointing away from the sun.

73

Earth Science
Core Skills Science, Grade 5

The shortest day of the year is the winter solstice on December 21 or 22. This marks the start of winter. The North Pole points directly *away* from the sun.

There are two equinoxes each year. On these days there is the same amount of sunlight and darkness everywhere on Earth. The vernal equinox is in March and marks the start of spring. The autumnal equinox is in September and marks the start of fall.

Seasons

All places on Earth have four seasons: spring, summer, fall, and winter. Not all places on Earth feel the seasons in the same way.

Near the poles, the sun's rays hit at sharp angles. These places, such as McMurdo, a research station in Antarctica, have cold weather all year long. Near the equator the sun's rays hit more directly. These places, such as Panama City, have mostly warm weather.

Some places feel the seasons more strongly. Chicago, Illinois, and Santiago, Chile, are about halfway between the equator and a pole. Their temperatures go up and down a lot. This shows that a place's position on Earth has a big effect on the place's weather and seasons.

Ideas About the Sun

Hundreds of years ago, people had ideas about the sun that were wrong. For example, people used to think that Earth was the center of the universe. They thought the sun revolved around Earth.

Galileo was an astronomer. An astronomer is a person who studies the skies. In the 1600s, he wrote a book that said that Earth revolved around the sun. He also explained why this happened. He was arrested for telling others about his idea.

Today, we know that Galileo was correct. Based on his work, scientists can tell where Earth, the sun, and other objects will appear in the sky.

People had other false ideas, too. They thought that the seasons came because of Earth's distance from the sun. We now know that Earth is actually closer to the sun in December than in June, so the Earth's closeness to the sun doesn't cause the seasons. We also know that the seasons are caused by Earth's tilted axis and revolutions around the sun. Because of the tilt, the sun rises higher in the sky. This makes summer days last longer.

What Causes Earth's Seasons?

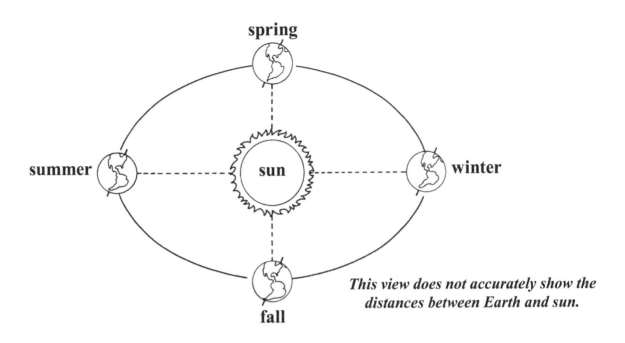

This view does not accurately show the distances between Earth and sun.

Fill in the blanks.

1. Seasons change as Earth _____ around the sun on its tilted axis.

2. When it is summer in the Northern Hemisphere, it is

   _____ in the Southern Hemisphere.

3. One full trip of the Earth around the sun is a(n) _____.

4. The longest day and the most light occur on the

   _____.

5. On the summer solstice, the North Pole tilts _____ the sun.

6. The shortest day and the least light occur on the

   _____.

7. Days equal in length occur on the vernal equinox and the

   _____.

8. Main Idea What causes day and night? What causes seasons?

_____

_____

9. Vocabulary Compare a solstice with an equinox. What seasons do these events mark?

_____

_____

10. Reading Skill: Cause and Effect Chicago, Illinois, lies midway between the North Pole and the equator. Why does Chicago have a wide range of yearly temperatures?

_____

_____

11. Critical Thinking: Apply Explain why summer in the Northern Hemisphere occurs when winter occurs in the Southern Hemisphere.

_____

_____

12. Inquiry Skill: Infer Why did people who lived hundreds of years ago think that the sun revolved around Earth?

_____

_____

13. Test Prep During an equinox, the number of hours of daylight is

    A greater than the number of hours of darkness.

    B less than the number of hours of darkness.

    C the same as the number of hours of darkness.

    D sometimes less than and sometimes greater than the number of hours of darkness.

Why Does the Moon Have Phases?

The moon revolves around Earth, and they revolve around the sun together. The same side of the moon always faces Earth, but the sun lights up different parts of the moon at different times.

The Moon

A satellite is an object that revolves around Earth. The moon is Earth's only natural satellite. The moon is a sphere, or round like a ball. It is much smaller than Earth, and it is 80 times lighter. Compared to Earth, the moon does not have a very strong gravitational pull. Because of this, there is not much of an atmosphere around the moon. Its gravity, though, is strong enough to affect Earth's tides.

Viewing the Moon

At night, the moon seems to be the biggest and brightest object in the sky. It is really much smaller than the other objects, though. It just looks large because it is so close to Earth. The planet Venus is about the same size as Earth. It looks like a small dot in the sky. Because the moon is closer to Earth, it looks much larger than Venus.

The moon looks bright at night. However, it does not produce any light. It looks bright because the sun is shining on it. That is why you can see the moon from Earth.

Like Earth, the moon rotates on an imaginary axis. One full rotation takes $27\frac{1}{3}$ days. The moon revolves around Earth. One revolution takes $27\frac{1}{3}$ days. Because the moon takes the same period of time to rotate and revolve, the same side of the moon always faces Earth.

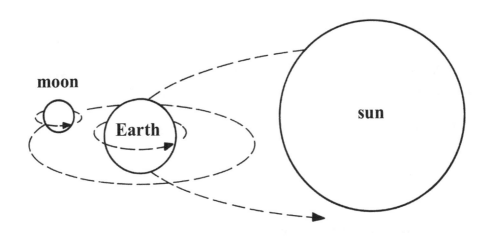

Phases of the Moon

The sun is always shining on the moon, so one half of the moon is always lit up. Because the moon revolves around Earth, the entire lighted half is not always visible. The shapes created by the changing amounts of the visible lighted areas are called moon phases. A complete cycle of moon phases takes about one month.

The first phase is the new moon, when the moon is between Earth and the sun. The lit side of the moon is facing away from Earth, so the moon appears dark.

As the moon continues to revolve around Earth, more of the lit area can be seen. The next phase is the waxing crescent. The moon appears to be waxing, or growing. When half the lit area can be seen, it is the first quarter phase. More and more of the moon is visible until the full moon phase is reached. Then the entire lit side can be seen.

The moon then appears to be waning, or getting smaller. Less of the lit side can be seen in the phases called waning gibbous, last quarter, and waning crescent.

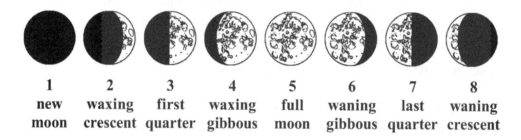

1	2	3	4	5	6	7	8
new moon	waxing crescent	first quarter	waxing gibbous	full moon	waning gibbous	last quarter	waning crescent

Eclipses

An eclipse occurs when one object passes into the shadow of another object. The moon's orbit is not in the same plane as Earth's orbit. Sometimes, however, the sun and the moon are lined up in a straight line. This can form two kinds of eclipses.

A solar eclipse takes place when the moon passes between the sun and Earth. The moon blocks the light from the sun. This makes a shadow on Earth.

The shadow has two parts. One part is darker than the other. The darker part of the shadow is the umbra. The part of Earth's surface within the umbra experiences a total solar eclipse. The lighter part of the shadow is the penumbra. The part of Earth's surface in the penumbra experiences a partial solar eclipse.

A lunar eclipse takes place when Earth passes directly between the sun and the moon. The moon then moves into Earth's shadow. A total lunar eclipse takes place when the entire moon passes into the umbra of Earth's shadow. The moon can still be seen during this time, but it has a reddish color. During a partial lunar eclipse, only part of the moon passes into the umbra. The rest of the moon is in the penumbra.

78

Name _____ Date _____

Why Does the Moon Have Phases?

Match each term to its description.

Terms

____ 1. moon phases

____ 2. waxing

____ 3. full moon

____ 4. waning

____ 5. eclipse

____ 6. umbra

____ 7. penumbra

Descriptions

a. when a decreasing area of the moon is lighted

b. the darker part of the shadow that forms during an eclipse

c. shapes created by the changing amounts of visible lighted areas of the moon

d. when one object passes into the shadow of another object

e. when an increasing area of the moon is lighted

f. the lighter part of the shadow that forms during an eclipse

g. the phase in which the entire side of the moon is visible from Earth

Look at the drawing. Then write answers to the questions on the lines below.

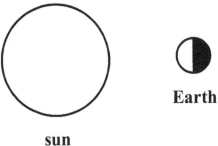

moon

Earth

sun

8. Which kind of eclipse occurs when Earth passes directly between the sun and the moon?

_____

_____

9. What condition exists during a lunar eclipse?

_____

_____

Earth Science
Core Skills Science, Grade 5

10. Main Idea Why is the same side of the moon always visible from Earth?

_____

_____

11. Vocabulary Explain what is meant by the term *moon phases*.

_____

_____

12. Reading Skill: Sequence List the sequence of the phases of the moon, starting with waxing gibbous and ending with the first quarter.

_____

_____

_____

13. Critical Thinking: Apply How would you determine what the phase of the moon will be 10 days from today?

_____

_____

14. Inquiry Skill: Compare Compare a solar eclipse with a lunar eclipse.

_____

_____

_____

15. Test Prep What happens during a total solar eclipse?

    A The moon blocks out all of the sun.

    B The sun blocks out all of the moon.

    C The moon blocks out part of the sun.

    D The sun blocks out part of the moon.

What Orbits the Sun?

The sun and the bodies that revolve, or travel, around it make up the solar system. Our solar system is huge, but it is only a tiny part of an enormous galaxy called the Milky Way.

The Sun and Its Neighbors

The solar system is made up of the sun and all the bodies that revolve around it. The solar system has eight planets, including Earth. A planet is a large body that revolves around the sun. Planets do not make their own light. They reflect light from the sun.

The sun is the largest part of the solar system. Some planets, like Mercury and Venus, can be seen from Earth by the naked eye. However, whether we can see these planets also depends on where they are in their orbits. They are not always visible. Many planets, like Earth, have one or more moons. The solar system also has asteroids, comets, and meteoroids.

The sun has strong gravity. The sun's gravity keeps all of the planets and objects traveling around the sun. The path that each object travels around the sun is called its orbit.

Moons

There are about 140 moons in the solar system. Moons are held in orbit by their planets' gravitational pull. Unlike Earth's moon, some moons have an atmosphere. Some seem to have water or ice beneath their surface. One has volcanoes.

Asteroids

An asteroid is a small, rocky object that orbits the sun. There are millions of them in the solar system. Most of them orbit in a band called the asteroid belt located between Mars and Jupiter. Asteroids can be hundreds of kilometers or only a few meters across.

81

Comets

A comet is a small orbiting body made of dust, ice, and frozen gases. Comets orbit the sun. The orbits of most comets are elliptical. This means that the comet passes close to the sun and then swings far away from it.

Comets have a cold center. The solid part of a comet is called the nucleus. When a comet comes near the sun, part of it starts to glow. This is called a coma. Energy from the sun makes the coma grow, and a glowing tail forms. The tail can be millions of kilometers long.

Some comets make one complete trip around the sun in fewer than 200 years. These are called short-period comets. Long-period comets travel much farther away from the sun. They may take 30 million years to orbit the sun!

Meteoroids

Orbiting the sun along with asteroids and comets are pieces of rock or metal called meteoroids. Many of these pieces of matter are probably the result of collisions between asteroids. Some pieces may have been part of comets that broke apart. Some meteoroids are large, like asteroids. Most are much smaller. Many are smaller than a grain of sand. When a meteoroid strikes Earth's atmosphere at high speed, the air is heated rapidly and releases energy. This forms a streak of light in the night sky called a meteor.

Sometimes many meteors can be seen at the same time. This is called a meteor shower. In some meteor showers, 50 meteors can be seen each hour. Meteor showers can last a few hours. Some last for a few days.

Meteoroids usually burn up as they fall through Earth's atmosphere. Sometimes a meteoroid does not burn up entirely and stays together. When it hits the ground, it is called a meteorite. Most meteorites seem to come from the asteroid belt.

Large meteorites can hit Earth's surface. When they do, they form impact craters. These are like large bowl-shaped holes on Earth.

What Orbits the Sun?

Write answers to the questions on the lines below.

1. What is a solar system?

   _____

2. What keeps the planets and other bodies in orbit around the sun?

   _____

3. What is a coma?

   _____

Label the nucleus and tail of the comet shown below.

4. _____   5. _____

6. What is the difference between a meteor and a meteoroid?

   _____

   _____

   _____

   _____

7. Main Idea What different types of bodies make up the solar system?

_____

8. Vocabulary Write a sentence correctly using the words *asteroid* and *comet*.

_____

_____

9. Reading Skill: Structure Make a brief outline that shows how these terms are related: *planets, moons, asteroids, the sun.*

10. Critical Thinking: Apply Earth and its moon formed at about the same time and from the same processes. Why do you think Earth's surface has fewer craters than the surface of the moon does?

_____

_____

11. Inquiry Skill: Research How could you find out more about collecting meteorites?

_____

_____

12. Test Prep Small rocky objects that orbit the sun between Mars and Jupiter are called

   A meteoroids.

   B meteorites.

   C comets.

   D asteroids.

What Are Elements?

Elements and Atoms

All matter is made up of elements, substances that cannot be broken apart into other substances. An atom is the smallest particle of an element that still has the properties of that element. Atoms are too small to be seen with a light microscope.

Organization of Atoms

Atoms contain negatively charged particles called electrons. Atoms also have a small core in the middle called the nucleus. Electrons move quickly around the nucleus, which is made of particles called protons and neutrons. Protons have a positive charge. Neutrons have no charge. The number of protons in an atom is usually the same as the number of electrons.

Atoms of a certain element all have the same number of protons in the nucleus, but the number of neutrons may vary.

Carbon is found in nature in many forms with different properties. This happens because carbon atoms can be put together in many different ways. Graphite, the "lead" in most pencils, is a form of carbon. The carbon atoms are grouped in rings of six atoms each.

Diamond is another form of pure carbon. It is the hardest natural substance on Earth because the carbon atoms are packed tightly together. No matter what form it takes, the element carbon is made up of atoms that all have the same number of protons.

Elements Alone and Joined

Most atoms join with other atoms to form molecules. A molecule is two or more atoms joined together by forces called chemical bonds. In a molecule, the atoms in some ways act together as one part. Some molecules are made up of one or more than one element. The oxygen in the air you breathe has two oxygen atoms. A molecule of water has two hydrogen atoms and one oxygen atom.

An element's properties come from the atoms that make up that element. Some properties are color, hardness, and density. The element copper is a shiny metal that can be stretched into wires. The element silver is a shiny metal that is soft enough to be formed into things like bracelets and rings. The element helium in balloons is less dense than air, causing the balloons to float. The element aluminum is a shiny metal. It is strong, but it does not weigh very much.

The Periodic Table

Scientists have named more than 100 elements. The elements are organized, or sorted out, in the periodic table.

Long ago, people in ancient Greece put forth the idea that all matter is made up of four elements: earth, air, fire, and water. But people began to understand that there must be more than just those four elements.

In the 1600s, an English scientist said that earth, air, fire, and water could not be real elements. In the late 1700s, a French scientist made one of the first lists of chemical elements.

By the 1800s, scientists had begun to name many new elements. They were also learning that some elements had properties that were alike. They began to organize elements into families, or groups, with properties that were alike. However, not all scientists grouped elements in the same way.

In 1869, Russian scientist Dmitri Mendeleev came up with a way to list and group the elements. He listed elements with similar properties together.

Today, scientists use a table called the periodic table. It is much like Mendeleev's table. It is called the periodic table because properties of the elements have a repeating pattern. *Periodic* means "repeating."

In the periodic table, elements are listed in order of increasing atomic number. This number tells how many protons are in an element's nucleus. The box for each element lists the atomic number, chemical symbol, and name. The chemical symbol is a shorter form of the element's name.

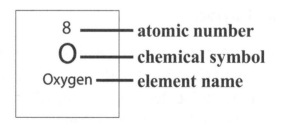

Classification of Elements

Colors on the periodic table show whether elements are metals, nonmetals, or metalloids. Metals are shiny, can be bent or stretched, and conduct electricity. Most elements are metals. Many nonmetals are gases. Solid nonmetals are usually dull in color. They do not conduct electricity, bend, or stretch very much. They break easily. Metalloids are like both metals and nonmetals.

Physical Science
Core Skills Science, Grade 5

What Are Elements?

Match each definition to its term.

Definitions

Terms

_____ 1. a substance that cannot be broken apart into other substances

a. electrons

b. nucleus

_____ 2. the smallest particle of an element that still has the properties of that element

c. proton

_____ 3. the negatively charged particles that make up part of every atom

d. molecule

e. neutron

_____ 4. the central core of an atom

f. element

_____ 5. a particle in the nucleus with a positive charge

g. atom

_____ 6. a particle in the nucleus with no charge

_____ 7. two or more atoms joined by chemical bonds

Fill in the blanks.

8. In 1869, Russian chemist Dmitri Mendeleev developed a way to classify

_____.

9. The modern periodic table is a table in which the elements are arranged by their

_____.

10. Elements are arranged in order of increasing _____ number, which is the number of protons in the nucleus.

11. The colors of the boxes show whether elements are _____,

_____, or _____.

12. _____ have properties of both metals and nonmetals.

Physical Science
Core Skills Science, Grade 5

13. Main Idea What are the tiny particles that make up an atom?

_____

14. Vocabulary What information about each element is contained in its box in the periodic table?

_____

_____

15. Reading Skill: Compare and Contrast Explain how diamond and graphite are similar and how they are different.

_____

_____

16. Critical Thinking: Analyze Suppose you are given a sample of an element. You are asked to identify the element as a metal or a nonmetal. What are some properties you would look for? Explain.

_____

_____

17. Inquiry Skill: Predict A uranium atom has 92 protons in its nucleus. Use what you know about atoms to predict how many electrons a uranium atom has.

_____

_____

18. Test Prep The properties of metalloids are

    A more like metals.

    B more like nonmetals.

    C somewhat like metals and somewhat like nonmetals.

    D somewhat like gases and somewhat like metals.

What Are Compounds?

Combining Elements

When two or more elements are chemically joined, they form a compound. Compounds, like elements, are pure substances. They have different properties from the elements that make them. In many compounds, atoms come together to form molecules. Each molecule of a compound has the same chemical properties.

At one time, people thought water was an element. However, an element cannot be broken down into other substances. Scientists figured out that water is not an element when they broke it down into other substances.

Water is a compound made of the elements hydrogen and oxygen. A compound is a substance made up of two or more elements that are chemically joined. Every molecule of water has two hydrogen atoms and one oxygen atom.

A compound has its own chemical properties. In many compounds, atoms come together to form molecules. Each molecule of a compound acts in the exact same way. They all have the same chemical properties.

All water molecules are made up of two hydrogen atoms and one oxygen atom. Every molecule of water has the properties of water. These properties are different from the properties of hydrogen and oxygen.

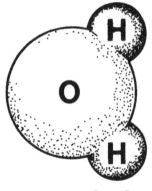
water molecule

Many Compounds

Many compounds are found in nature, and many are made of two elements. When you breathe out, your breath contains a compound called carbon dioxide. Molecules of carbon dioxide are made up of one carbon atom and two oxygen atoms.

Rust is a compound called iron oxide. It is made of iron and oxygen. When iron joins with oxygen in the air, rust forms. Water makes this change happen even faster.

© Houghton Mifflin Harcourt Publishing Company

Physical Science
Core Skills Science, Grade 5

Making and Breaking Compounds

To form a compound, atoms of the elements in the compound must take part in a chemical reaction. A chemical reaction is a process in which one or more substances are changed into one or more different substances.

Energy is an important part of all chemical reactions. Energy is needed to break apart compounds. When elements join to form compounds, energy is let go.

Compounds and Formulas

A chemical formula is a short way to describe a chemical compound. Chemical formulas use chemical symbols to show which elements are in a compound. For example, the chemical symbol for iron is Fe. The chemical symbol for sulfur is S. The chemical formula for iron sulfide is FeS. There is one iron atom for every sulfur atom.

Often a compound has more of one element than another element. A number in the chemical formula tells you how many atoms of that element are in the compound. The chemical formula for water is H_2O. This means that there are two hydrogen atoms for every one oxygen atom.

Water

Water is everywhere on Earth. About three-fourths of Earth's surface is covered with water. All forms of life depend on water to live.

Water is different from other compounds. It is one of the few compounds that is liquid at room temperature. It is also able to dissolve, or break down, more substances than any other liquid.

One reason water has these properties is because of the shape of its molecules. Water molecules have a bent shape. This gives the oxygen end of the molecule a bit of a negative charge and the hydrogen end a bit of a positive charge. These differences make water able to dissolve many compounds.

The charges also draw the hydrogen and oxygen ends of different water molecules together. This is why water is a liquid at many temperatures.

90

Name _____ Date _____

What Are Compounds?

Write answers to the questions on the lines below.

1. What is a compound?

   _____

   _____

2. What happens during a chemical reaction?

   _____

   _____

3. What is the chemical formula that has two hydrogen atoms and one oxygen atom?

   _____

4. What elements does the compound iron oxide (Fe_2O_3) have?

   _____

   _____

5. What is needed to create chemical reactions?

   _____

   _____

6. What unique properties does the compound water have?

   _____

Carbon
Dioxide
CO_2

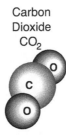

Physical Science
Core Skills Science, Grade 5

7. Main Idea Why can elements be called the building blocks of matter?

_____

_____

8. Vocabulary In your own words, define *chemical formula*.

_____

_____

9. Reading Skill: Compare and Contrast How are elements and compounds alike? How are they different?

_____

_____

_____

10. Critical Thinking: Apply Research some compounds other than the ones mentioned in this lesson. Pick one example and explain how you know it is a compound.

_____

_____

11. Inquiry Skill: Infer Ty added water to a mixture of two other substances. A short time later, he observed that one substance had turned green and another had turned orange. What might Ty infer?

_____

_____

12. Test Prep Elements and compounds

   A are pure substances.

   B are made up of atoms.

   C have specific properties.

   D are all of the above.

How Can Materials Be Identified?

Using Your Senses

Every kind of material is some form of matter with specific properties, or traits. Properties can be used to help identify pure substances like elements and compounds and to tell one kind of matter from another.

Two kinds of properties can be used to describe and group matter—physical properties and chemical properties. Think about a sheet of paper and a sheet of tin foil. Both are thin, flat, and bend easily. These are physical properties. Also note that paper will burn and tin will not. Burning is a chemical property.

A physical property can be measured or noticed by the senses. Some physical properties are state, size, color, and smell. Many physical properties, such as volume, mass, and density, can be measured.

A chemical property is the ability of a material to change its chemical makeup. Materials are made of much smaller parts—atoms and molecules. When there are changes in the way that the atoms and molecules are put together, a new material is formed. The new material has different properties from the first material.

You can discover a material's chemical properties by noticing how it changes when different things happen to it. When a piece of paper is held in a flame, the paper will burn. Burning is a chemical change in which matter joins with oxygen. Burning paper makes new matter that is very different from the paper and oxygen.

Mass, Volume, and Density

Mass is a measure of the amount of matter in an object or material. It can be measured on a scale in grams (g) or kilograms (kg). A large object has more matter, and more mass, than a smaller object of the same material.

Volume is the amount of space matter takes up. The volume of a solid can be measured in cubic centimeters (cm^3). Liquid volumes can be measured in liters (L) or milliliters (mL). One cubic centimeter equals one milliliter. You can find the volume of a rectangular solid by multiplying its length, width, and height.

Density is not the same as mass. The density of a material is its mass per unit volume. To find the density of a material, divide the measurement of mass by the volume.

All amounts of an element or compound that are kept in the same way have the same density. That means that a drop of pure water and a large amount of pure water both have a density of 1 g/mL. This is the density of pure liquid water. Liquids with other densities are not pure water.

Melting and Boiling Points

State of matter is another physical property. The three states of matter are solid, liquid, and gas.

Solids are firm. They have an exact shape and volume. Liquids flow. They take on the shape of their container but keep the same volume. Gases have no real shape or volume. They can move and fill any container.

When enough energy is added to a solid, it melts to make a liquid. The temperature at which a solid changes to a liquid is its melting point. When enough energy is taken away from a liquid, it freezes to make a solid. A substance always has the same freezing point and the same melting point. When enough energy is added to a liquid, it changes to a gas. The temperature at which this happens is its boiling point.

Solubility

The measure of how much of one substance can dissolve in another is called solubility, another physical property of matter. Some substances are very soluble in water but not in other liquids, such as alcohol.

Conductivity

Another physical property of matter is conductivity. The conductivity of a material is its ability to carry energy. Electrical conductivity has to do with carrying electricity. Thermal conductivity has to do with carrying heat.

Most metals are good conductors of both electricity and heat. Copper is used both in pots and pans and in electrical wires.

Materials that have low conductivity, such as rubber and plastic, are used to protect conductors. In an electric cord, plastic around the metal wire keeps the electricity and heat from leaving.

94

Name _____ Date _____

How Can Materials Be Identified?

Fill in the blanks.

1. A characteristic that can be measured or detected by the senses is called a(n)

   _____.

2. A(n) _____ is the ability of a material to change its chemical makeup.

3. Mass is a measure of the amount of _____ in an object or material.

4. Cubic centimeters (cm³), liters (L), and milliliters (mL) are units used to measure

   _____, or the amount of space a sample of matter takes up.

5. Pure water has a(n) _____, or mass per unit volume, of 1 g/mL.

6. The temperature at which a solid substance changes to a(n)

   _____ substance is known as the melting point.

7. The boiling point of a substance is the temperature at which it changes from a liquid

   to a(n) _____.

8. The measure of how much of one substance can dissolve in another substance is

   called _____.

9. _____ is the ability of a material to carry energy.

10. Electrical conductivity refers to carrying electricity, and

    _____ conductivity refers to carrying heat.

Physical Science
Core Skills Science, Grade 5

11. Main Idea How are physical and chemical properties of matter useful?

_____

_____

12. Vocabulary How is the density of a substance related to its mass and its volume?

_____

_____

13. Reading Skill: Main Idea and Details What can you conclude about two liquid samples that have different boiling points?

_____

_____

14. Critical Thinking: Apply You should not swim outdoors during a thunderstorm. A lightning strike could send an electric charge through the water to your body. Which physical property of water explains this safety tip?

_____

_____

15. Inquiry Skill: Infer What is the volume, in milliliters, of a rectangular solid that has a length of 3 cm, a width of 2 cm, and a height of 2 cm?

_____

_____

16. Test Prep Which of the following is not a physical property of matter?

    A conductivity

    B density

    C reactivity

    D solubility

What Are Solutions and Mixtures?

Some mixtures are evenly mixed. Other mixtures have different amounts of materials in different places. Mixtures whose molecules are evenly mixed are called solutions.

Types of Mixtures

Look at the salad below. Each vegetable adds to its good taste. Yet if you ate different parts of the salad, you would taste each vegetable by itself. That is because a salad is a mixture. A mixture is a physical combination of two or more substances. The substances in a mixture are not chemically joined as they are in a compound. Even when their properties do react or change, the substances maintain the same total mass.

Mixtures are heterogeneous or homogeneous. In a heterogeneous mixture, such as a salad, materials are not spread out evenly. Separate pieces are in some parts of the mixture but not in others. A homogeneous mixture is the same all the way through. A sample of one part of the mixture is the same as every other sample from the mixture.

In a mixture, each part keeps its own properties. If you separated all the parts of a salad, the tomatoes would still be tomatoes, and so on.

Mixture or Compound?

Mixtures that are alike can be made of the same materials, but in different amounts. Two salads can both have lettuce and carrots, but one might have more carrots than the other. Two of the same compounds, however, always have the same materials in the same amounts.

Solutions

A solution is a homogeneous mixture, meaning that two or more substances are spread evenly throughout the mixture. The atoms or molecules of the materials mix together.

You make a solution when you make lemonade from a powdered mix. Some particles that mix in the water are molecules of sugar and coloring.

In any solution, the substance being dissolved is the solute. The substance that dissolves the solute is the solvent. In a solution of water and sugar, water is the solvent and sugar is the solute. In a solution, the properties of the substances that make up the mixtures do not change and the substances' total mass doesn't change, either.

97

Many solutions have a liquid solvent and a solid solute. However, solutions can have other kinds of solvents and solutes. Soda water is a solution made of carbon dioxide gas dissolved in water. Air is a solution of different gases. Brass is a solution of two solids—zinc and copper.

Particles in a solution spread evenly through the solution because they mix at the level of their atoms or molecules. When iodine and alcohol are mixed, the iodine dissolves in the alcohol. The particles of iodine spread all through the mixture. The molecules of the two substances have become evenly mixed.

Separating a Solution

To separate a solution, use the properties of the mixed materials. The size of the particles does not help because they are so small, and it is hard to trap and separate them.

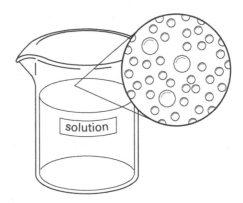

solution

You can use other properties. You can allow a liquid solvent to evaporate and leave the solute behind. A simple way to separate most solutions is to use different boiling or melting points of the substance. Sugar is gathered in this way. Sugar cane plants are cut down, and the stems are crushed. The sugar cane juice is heated. The water boils off, leaving solid sugar behind.

Alloys

Mixtures of two or more metals are called alloys, which may also be mixtures of a metal and another solid. Alloys often have some of the properties of each material that forms them.

Bronze is an alloy of copper and tin. It has the best properties of both metals. Bronze is a strong alloy. It is also easy to hammer into thin sheets that can be formed into different shapes.

The amounts of each material in an alloy can change its properties. Steel is an alloy of iron, carbon, and other solids. Softer steel is made with less carbon. Harder steel is made with more carbon.

Name _____ Date _____

What Are Solutions and Mixtures?

Fill in the blanks with the correct terms.

1. A(n) _____ is a physical combination of two or more substances.

2. Complete the following diagram.

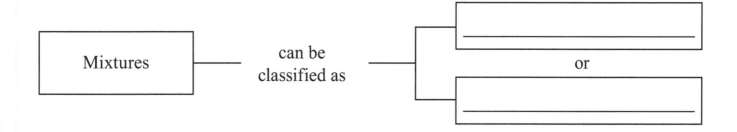

3. Each part of a mixture keeps its original _____.

4. Unlike a compound, the composition of a mixture can _____.

5. Complete the following diagram.

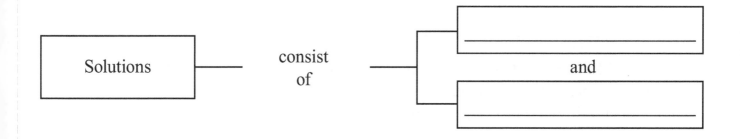

6. Because the substances of a solution are evenly distributed throughout the mixture,

    a solution is said to be _____.

7. The substance being dissolved in a solution is called the _____.

8. An alloy is a mixture of two or more _____.

Physical Science
Core Skills Science, Grade 5

9. **Main Idea** How are solutions different from other mixtures?

_____

_____

_____

10. **Vocabulary** How do solutes differ from solvents? Include a specific solution in your answer.

_____

_____

11. **Reading Skill: Draw Conclusions** A mixture is made up of evenly spaced atoms of copper and silver. Is the mixture a solution? Explain your answer.

_____

_____

12. **Critical Thinking: Apply** Mia makes a delicious soup broth. She wants to separate the solid ingredients from the broth. How could she do this?

_____

_____

13. **Inquiry Skill: Predict** A student has jars containing different amounts of water. She adds salt to each jar until no more salt will dissolve. She makes the chart below. Predict how much salt will dissolve in 100 mL of water.

Water	25 mL	50 mL	75 mL	100 mL
Salt	9 g	18 g	27 g	?

14. **Test Prep** Which of the following is a type of alloy?

    A salt water

    B gold

    C iodine

    D bronze

What Are the Three States of Matter?

A state of matter is the physical form that matter takes. Three states of matter are solids, liquids, and gases. All matter is made up of atoms and molecules. These particles are always moving. The state of matter depends on the movement and spacing of these particles.

For most solids, particles are held closely together and do not move around one another. In liquids, particles are close together, but they have space in which to move past one another. In gases, particles are spread far apart. Their arrangements have no order, and they bounce off each other and the sides of their containers.

Solids

A solid is a form of matter that has a definite shape and volume. The way that particles in solids are arranged and the way they move back-and-forth in place gives solids their properties. One property is that solids keep their shape. If you move a solid or place it into a container, its shape will stay the same. Wood is a solid. A block of wood will keep its shape wherever you put it.

Particles in a solid are very close together, so it is hard to compress, or squeeze, them. This is why the shape of a solid does not change.

Another property of solids is that they have definite volume. That is, they take up the same amount of space wherever they are placed. The volume of a solid object stays the same unless you remove a part of the object.

Many solids might seem to change shape and volume. For example, you can squeeze a foam ball into a smaller volume. A pillow changes shape when you rest your head on it. In both cases, however, solid matter is surrounded by "pockets" of air. The air changes its shape and volume. The solid parts do not.

Liquids

What shape is orange juice? You cannot say, because orange juice is a liquid. A liquid is a form of matter that has a definite volume but no definite shape. A liquid will change its shape to match the shape of its container. Think about what happens when you use a straw to drink orange juice from a container. The juice has one shape in the container and a different shape when it is in the straw.

Like solids, each liquid has a volume that does not change. Think about pouring a liquid into bottles of different shapes. Each time, the liquid takes on the shape of the bottle, but the liquid's volume never changes. Liquids are not easy to compress or squeeze. Because the molecules are close together, liquids do not squeeze into smaller volumes very easily.

Gases

A gas is a form of matter that has no definite shape or volume. The particles in gases move around freely and bounce off one another. When a gas is placed in a closed container, the particles spread out to fill the container. They take the shape of the container. Gas particles are easy to compress, so they can be squeezed into a smaller volume.

Changes of State

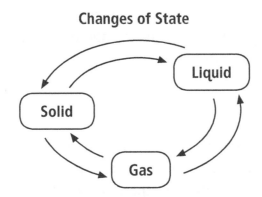

To understand how gases are compressed and take the shape of containers, think about helium gas. Helium gas is often compressed inside a metal tank. It takes the shape and volume of the tank. If you use the helium to fill balloons, the gas takes on the different shapes and volumes of the balloons.

Changes of State

Matter can change from one state to another when energy is added or removed. Changes of states are always physical changes.

When energy is added to a solid, its temperature rises to a certain point. When the substance reaches its melting point, the solid melts, changing from a solid to a liquid.

When enough energy is added to a substance, a liquid is vaporized. Vaporization changes a liquid to a gas. Rapid vaporization is called boiling. The boiling point of a substance is the temperature at which it boils. Slow vaporization is called evaporation, which takes place on a liquid's surface. When energy is taken from a gas, condensation occurs. Condensation is a change of state from a gas to a liquid.

Skipping a Step

Sometimes matter skips the liquid state! The process of changing from a solid to a gas is called sublimation. For example, "dry ice" is made of solid carbon dioxide, which does not melt into a liquid but becomes a gas when it heats up.

The opposite of sublimation is deposition, the change of state from a gas to a solid. When water vapor touches freezing cold surfaces, it changes into a solid called frost.

Name _____ Date _____

What Are the Three States of Matter?

Fill in the blanks.

1. The physical form that matter takes, such as solid, liquid, and gas, is called

   _____.

2. For most substances, particles are most _____ packed in the solid state.

3. A(n) _____ is a form of matter that has a definite shape and volume.

4. A(n) _____ is a form of matter that has a definite volume, but no definite shape.

5. A(n) _____ is a form of matter that has no definite shape or volume.

6. What happens when energy is removed from a liquid?

   _____

   _____

7. What happens in evaporation?

   _____

   _____

8. What happens in sublimation?

   _____

   _____

9. What happens in deposition?

   _____

   _____

10. Main Idea What two factors determine the state of matter of an object or sample?

_____

_____

11. Vocabulary Describe the processes of vaporization and condensation.

_____

_____

_____

12. Reading Skill: Cause and Effect When will a liquid evaporate, and when will it boil? Compare the two changes.

_____

_____

13. Critical Thinking: Evaluate Why must a gas be kept in a closed container?

_____

_____

14. Inquiry Skill: Observe A solid has undergone a physical change. What observations can you make to determine which change of state took place?

_____

_____

_____

15. Test Prep Solids and liquids are similar because both

A are fluids.

B are compressible.

C have no definite shape.

D have definite volume.

What Can Change an Object's Motion?

Motion and Newton's First Law

Motion is a change in an object's position. A motionless object is at rest, or stationary. Sir Isaac Newton described several laws in 1867 that explain much about motion. His laws show how forces and motion are connected. A force is a push or pull that acts on an object. Even when an object is stationary, it has multiple balancing forces acting upon it. But because these forces are balanced, the object doesn't move.

Newton's first law of motion states that an object at rest remains at rest. An outside force must act on it to make it move. Likewise, an object in motion stays in motion. The resistance to a change in motion is called inertia.

Speed, Velocity, and Acceleration

Newton's first law explains that an outside force is needed to change an object's speed or direction. Speed is a measure of distance moved in a given amount of time.

To calculate average speed, divide the distance traveled by the time it took the object to travel that distance. You can use this formula to relate speed (s), distance (d), and time (t):

$$s = d/t$$

If a car travels 160 miles in 2 hours, the average speed is

$$s = 160 \; mi/2 \; h$$
$$s = 80 \; mph$$

There are many other units of speed. However, they are all written as units of distance per units of time. Meters per second (m/s) is one common unit.

Top Animal Speeds

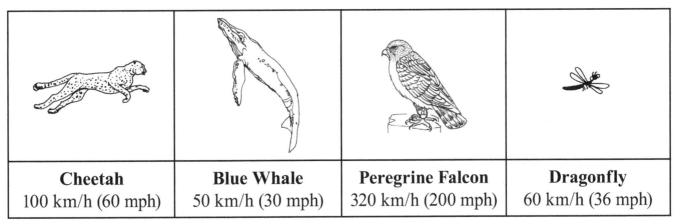

Cheetah	Blue Whale	Peregrine Falcon	Dragonfly
100 km/h (60 mph)	50 km/h (30 mph)	320 km/h (200 mph)	60 km/h (36 mph)

Velocity is a measure of both an object's speed and its direction. If you and a friend both run at a speed of 5 mph but go in different directions, you have different velocities.

Whenever an object's speed or direction changes, its velocity changes, too. This change is called acceleration. Acceleration measures a change in speed, in direction, or both over a certain amount of time. Acceleration is written as units of distance per units of time squared, or m/s^2.

Newton's Second Law

Imagine you and a friend are pulling on opposite ends of a rope. You are pulling with greater force. The difference between the two forces is called net force.

Newton's second law of motion states that an object accelerates, or changes its motion, only when an unbalanced force acts on it. The law can be written as a formula:

$$F = ma$$

F is the applied net force, m is the mass of the object, and a is the amount of acceleration. Force is measured in a unit called the newton (N). One newton is the force required to accelerate a mass of 1 kg at 1 meter per second squared.

Gravity

Gravity is a force that causes objects with mass to be attracted, or pulled, toward one another. Gravity is a noncontact force because it acts on an object without touching it. According to Newton, gravity increases with the masses of two objects. As the objects get farther apart, gravity pulls with weaker force. Earth's mass is much greater than the mass of any object, so gravity pulls all objects toward Earth's center.

Friction

Friction is a force that resists motion of one surface across another surface. Friction is a contact force because objects or surfaces touch one another. Friction is usually greater between rough surfaces than smooth ones.

In the picture, the slowing force of friction happens between the ground and the skate wheels. If the skater uses his brakes, friction increases. He will stop sooner. Air resistance, or drag, will also help slow down the skater. This kind of friction resists motion through air.

106

What Can Change an Object's Motion?

Fill in the blanks.

1. _____ is a change in an object's position.

2. A(n) _____ is a push or a pull that acts on an object.

3. The tendency of an object at rest to remain at rest or an object in motion to remain

   in motion is called _____.

4. Velocity is a measure of both an object's speed and its

   _____.

5. The average speed of a car that travels 100 miles in 4 hours is

   _____.

6. The difference between a greater force and a weaker force is

   _____.

7. One _____ is the force required to accelerate a mass of
   1kg at 1m/s per second.

8. A noncontact force that causes objects with mass to be attracted toward one another

   is _____.

9. _____ is a contact force that resists the motion of one surface
   across another surface.

10. **Main Idea** How can an object's speed or direction be changed?

   _____

   _____

11. Vocabulary What is the difference between velocity and acceleration? Give an example of each. Be sure to use the correct units.

_____

_____

12. Reading Skill: Main Idea and Details What are three ways an object may accelerate?

_____

_____

13. Critical Thinking: Analyze Explain why the shoulder strap of a car seat belt is important.

_____

_____

_____

14. Inquiry Skill: Measure In the United States, speed is typically measured in mph. To convert mph to km/h, multiply by 1.6. Calculate in km/h the speed of a train traveling 75 mph.

_____

15. Test Prep The brakes on a bicycle slow it down due to the force of

   A acceleration.

   B air resistance.

   C gravity.

   D friction.

How Are Sounds Made?

Mechanical Waves

A mechanical wave forms when a disturbance causes energy to travel through matter, such as air, water, or another medium. Mechanical waves can move only through matter. They cannot move through empty space.

Mechanical waves move in different ways. A transverse wave moves perpendicular to the direction that the medium moves. Part of the wave moves up as energy moves through it. As that part drops back down, it sends energy to the next part. Then that part moves up. The wave moves left to right.

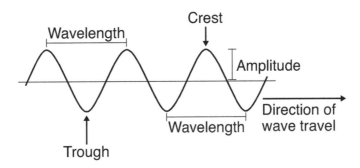

Mechanical waves can also move as longitudinal waves. Particles move back and forth parallel to the direction the wave travels. A spring snapping back and forth creates longitudinal waves. Compression happens wherever particles in a longitudinal wave come together. Rarefaction happens wherever particles spread out.

Mechanical waves can interact, or share space with, other waves. When two waves cross paths, they can combine to form a new wave, add to each other, or cancel each other out. Their interaction depends on the height or position of each wave at that point in time. The waves return to normal once they pass each other by. That's why you can sometimes hear two different sounds at the same time without getting them mixed up.

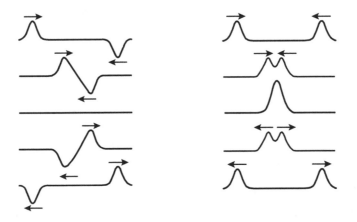

109

Scientists measure wave amplitude, wavelength, and frequency. Amplitude is the height of the crests or troughs from the rest position of a transverse wave. Wavelength is the distance between two neighboring crests or troughs. Frequency is the number of waves that pass a point per second.

Sound Waves

Sound waves are a type of longitudinal mechanical wave. Sound waves happen due to vibrations, or rapid back-and-forth movement of an object. Vibrations compress and spread apart the air molecules around them. The first molecules bump into other molecules. Then those molecules bump into other ones. In this way, sound waves spread out.

The tuba is a musical instrument. The tuba makes sound when air travels through it. When the player's lips vibrate, the air inside the tuba vibrates, too. The vibrating air moves through the instrument. This makes the metal vibrate. The sound that comes out is magnified.

Pitch

Objects vibrate and create sound waves with different properties. Pitch is how low or high you sense the sound to be. Pitch depends on the sound wave's frequency. The higher the frequency, the higher the pitch of the sound.

Volume

Volume is how loud or soft a sound is. It is a measure of the intensity, or strength, of the vibrations that lead to sound. The amplitude of the sound waves determines intensity. Hearing loud sounds continuously can damage hearing.

Acoustics

Sound waves act in different ways when they move from one medium into another. When a sound wave strikes a surface, several things can happen. Sound may reflect off the surface. For example, sound waves hitting a hard surface like concrete will be bounced off. Sound waves can pass through a surface. Or the surface may absorb the sound. Acoustics is the study of how materials affect sound waves.

How Are Sounds Made?

Fill in the blanks in the diagram using the terms **parallel,** *perpendicular, transverse wave, longitudinal wave, rarefaction,* and *compression.*

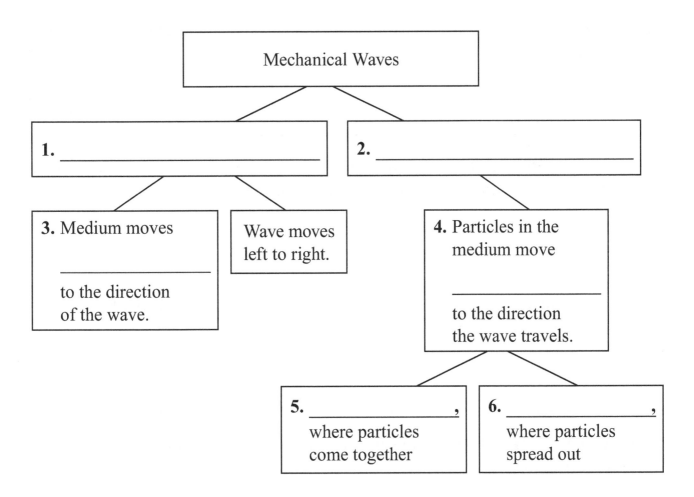

Match each definition to its term.

Definitions   **Terms**

_____ **7.** number of waves that pass a point per second   **a.** frequency

_____ **8.** how high or low a sound is perceived to be   **b.** acoustics

_____ **9.** how loud or soft a sound is   **c.** pitch

_____**10.** study of how materials affect sound waves   **d.** volume

Name _____ Date _____

11. Main Idea What are sound waves and how do they travel?

_____

_____

12. Vocabulary What are vibrations? Give an example of an object that vibrates and describe the effect of the vibrations.

_____

_____

13. Reading Skill: Draw Conclusions Why is it important to wear ear protection if you are working with a loud device such as a jackhammer?

_____

_____

14. Critical Thinking: Synthesize What effect can materials around your home stereo have on the music you play?

_____

_____

15. Inquiry Skill: Hypothesize How might sound reflect off a hard, curved surface? Propose a hypothesis.

_____

_____

_____

16. Test Prep Waves observed moving up and down are examples of

    A longitudinal waves.

    B transverse waves.

    C compression waves.

    D electromagnetic waves.

What Are Some Properties of Light?

Electromagnetic Waves

Mechanical waves, such as sound waves, can only pass through matter, such as air or water. Electromagnetic waves can travel through a vacuum as well as matter. Electromagnetic waves include gamma rays, x-rays, ultraviolet rays, visible light, infrared rays, microwaves, and radio waves. These waves fall along the electromagnetic spectrum from shorter wavelengths to longer wavelengths.

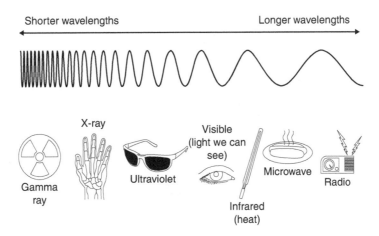

Visible light is electromagnetic radiation that people can see. It is in the middle of the spectrum and can be split into different colors.

The sun and other stars give off all the wavelengths of electromagnetic waves. Some of these waves are harmful to life on Earth, but Earth's atmosphere blocks many of them.

Ultraviolet radiation in sunlight does reach Earth's surface. This radiation can burn your skin and cause skin cancer. Wearing sunscreen helps protect against this radiation.

Reflection

Electromagnetic waves act in different ways when they hit different materials. Sometimes the waves are absorbed and changed into thermal energy. Other wavelengths are reflected. Reflection occurs when a wave bounces off a surface. Light reflecting from objects is what makes them visible.

A mirror is coated with metal that reflects almost all light that shines on it. When you look at a mirror, you see all the different wavelengths of light reflected. It is almost like looking at the object itself.

Light waves move at different speeds through different mediums. When light waves pass from one medium into another, they often change speed. As it changes speed, light refracts, or bends.

113

Physical Science
Core Skills Science, Grade 5

Refraction

Refraction takes place when the path of a light wave changes as it moves from one medium to another. For example, look at the picture of the pencil in the glass. The pencil appears to be broken, but it is not. Light travels at different speeds through water, glass, and air. The light waves refract, or bend, as they pass through each medium, so images can appear bent or broken.

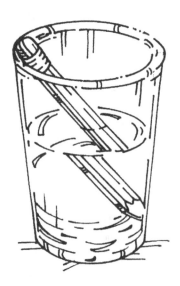

How can refraction be put to good use? Tools that refract light include eyeglasses, contact lenses, cameras, microscopes, and telescopes.

All these tools use lenses. A lens is a curved piece of clear material that refracts light in a controlled way. It refracts light to create useful images. A convex lens is thicker at the center than at its edges. It bends light rays toward one another. A concave lens is thinner at its center. It bends light rays away from one another.

Your eyes have lenses to help them see. In an eye that sees perfectly, the lens focuses images onto a part called the retina. If an image forms just in front of or behind the retina, vision is blurry. Glasses or contact lenses correct vision. They bend light rays just enough to focus the image correctly.

By combining convex and concave lenses in different ways, people can make many different tools. For example, many telescopes use two convex lenses to make faraway objects look larger. Microscopes use lenses to make small objects appear larger.

Fiber Optics

Reflection of light makes the use of fiber optics possible. In fiber optics, special fibers carry light waves along a cable that bends. The development of fiber optics has made it easier to communicate over the telephone and the Internet.

Name _____ Date _____

What Are Some Properties of Light?

Write answers to the questions on the lines below.

1. What determines where electromagnetic waves fall on the electromagnetic spectrum?

_____

_____

2. Give three examples of electromagnetic waves.

_____

_____

3. What is visible light?

_____

_____

4. What electromagnetic wave can damage the skin?

_____

_____

5. Give three examples of tools that use refracted light.

_____

_____

6. What is a lens?

_____

_____

115

Physical Science
Core Skills Science, Grade 5

Name _____ Date _____

7. **Main Idea** How are electromagnetic waves different from mechanical waves?

_____

_____

8. **Vocabulary** Write a sentence about light using the terms *reflection* and *refraction*.

_____

_____

9. **Reading Skill: Cause and Effect** What causes light to refract? Give an example from everyday life.

_____

_____

_____

10. **Critical Thinking: Apply** What might cause an overhead projector image to be out of focus? How might you correct the problem?

_____

_____

11. **Inquiry Skill: Analyze Data** On the electromagnetic spectrum, electromagnetic waves appear from left to right, from shorter wavelengths to longer wavelengths. Based on the diagram data in the reading, which electromagnetic waves have the longest wavelength?

_____

_____

12. **Test Prep** Electromagnetic waves differ from mechanical waves in that they

   A can be reflected.

   B contain less energy.

   C can travel through a vacuum.

   D can travel through matter.

What Is Thermal Energy?

Temperature and Thermal Energy

All matter is made up of tiny particles, such as atoms and molecules. These particles are always moving, so they make kinetic energy. Thermal energy is the total kinetic energy of the particles within a material.

The particles of a hot liquid move faster than the particles of a cold liquid. Faster particles have more kinetic energy. The words "hot" and "cold" refer to temperature. Temperature is a measure of the average kinetic energy of particles within a material.

Thermometers have temperature scales. Units on the scale are called degrees. Most people in the United States prefer the Fahrenheit scale. People in the rest of the world and people who work in science use the Celsius scale. Water freezes at 32°F or 0°C. Water boils at 212°F or 100°C.

Heat

Thermal energy is made when other forms of energy go through a change. Thermal energy can move through matter. The movement of thermal energy from warmer parts of matter to cooler parts is called heat.

An urn is a large metal container with a faucet, used for making hot beverages. An urn of hot cocoa and a cup of cocoa from the urn have the same temperature. But the urn of cocoa contains more cocoa, so it has more particles in motion and therefore more thermal energy than the cocoa in the cup. Cocoa in the cup has less thermal energy, so it cools faster.

Thermal energy always passes from warmer matter to cooler matter. Imagine you are holding an ice cube. Your hand is warmer than the ice cube. When thermal energy moves from your hand and to the ice cube, the ice cube gets warmer and starts to melt. The hand gets cold because it loses thermal energy. Cold does not pass from the ice cube to the hand.

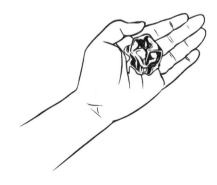

Physical Science
Core Skills Science, Grade 5

Conduction

Transfer of thermal energy through direct contact is called conduction. Conduction happens mainly in solids. Particles vibrate, or move back and forth. They bump into other particles and pass some of their kinetic energy to them. Those particles start to move. Thermal energy is spread throughout the object. This is also how it spreads among solid objects that are touching.

Convection

How thermal energy spreads through liquids and gases is called convection. The temperature of a gas or liquid rises when a hot object touches it. Warm, light liquids rise, while cold, dense liquids sink. This process is called convection.

Radiation

Thermal energy can also be transferred by radiation. Radiation is the transfer of energy by electromagnetic waves. All objects give off thermal radiation. When an object absorbs thermal radiation, its particles vibrate faster. Their kinetic energy increases, and their temperature rises.

The most important source of radiation for Earth is the sun. The sun gives off radiation of different wavelengths. Some are waves of visible light. Others are infrared light. They have a longer wavelength. Infrared radiation gives the sun most of its heating power. We depend on the sun for light and heat. Likewise, a campfire radiates helpful light and heat.

Ultraviolet (UV) rays have shorter wavelengths than visible light. Earth's upper atmosphere blocks some, but not all, UV rays. If your skin absorbs too much UV radiation, you get sunburned. You should wear sunscreen. It helps block UV rays.

Conductors and Insulators

A conductor is a material that easily transfers thermal energy. Solids are usually better conductors than liquids or gases. The particles in solids are close together, so vibrations pass more easily among them. Most metals are excellent heat conductors, but some solids, like wood, conduct heat slowly.

An insulator is a poor conductor of heat. Insulators, such as blankets, trap the energy your body makes and help keep you warm. Air and man-made materials such as fiberglass insulation trap heat to keep your home warm.

What Is Thermal Energy?

Write answers to the questions on the lines below.

1. What causes an ice cube to melt?

   _____

   _____

2. Which temperature scale is commonly used in the United States?

   _____

3. What is temperature?

   _____

   _____

4. What is heat?

   _____

   _____

Match each definition to its term.

Definitions   **Terms**

____ 5. transfer of thermal energy through direct contact   **a.** convection

____ 6. transfer of thermal energy through the flow of air   **b.** insulator
      or liquids
                                                         c. radiation

____ 7. transfer of thermal energy by electromagnetic waves

____ 8. a material that transfers thermal energy better than   **d.** conduction
      other materials
                                                     e. conductor

____ 9. a material that resists the transfer of thermal energy

Physical Science
Core Skills Science, Grade 5

10. Main Idea Name and describe the three ways that thermal energy is transferred.

_____

_____

11. Vocabulary What is the difference between *conduction* and *convection*?

_____

_____

12. Reading Skill: Compare and Contrast How does the thermal energy of a tub full of hot water compare to that of a glass of water at the same temperature? Explain.

_____

_____

13. Critical Thinking: Apply How might you determine if a material is a conductor or an insulator?

_____

_____

14. Inquiry Skill: Infer Why does water's freezing point make water a poor choice for the liquid in a thermometer?

_____

_____

15. Test Prep When an ice cube is placed in a glass of water, thermal energy

   A increases.

   B moves from the ice to the water.

   C moves from the water to the ice.

   D decreases.

How Is Electricity Produced?

Static and Current Electricity

Rub a balloon against your hair. Your hair rises up to meet the balloon because of static electricity. Static electricity is an electric force between nonmoving electric charges.

When you rub a balloon against your hair, the balloon now has extra electrons. So, it takes on an overall negative charge. Because the balloon has taken some of the electrons from the hair, the hair is left with a positive charge. Your positively charged hair is attracted to the negatively charged balloon and starts to rise up to meet it.

Charged objects apply a force on one another. Two objects with the same charges repel, or push away from, each other. Two objects with opposite charges attract, or pull toward, each other.

Have you ever walked across a thick carpet and then touched a metal doorknob? You might have felt a mild shock! You might have even seen a spark. Static electricity was being discharged, or released. Electrons moved between you and the doorknob. Lightning is a great big spark of static electricity! It has a lot of energy. But it lasts a very short time.

Batteries and Fuel Cells

A battery contains one or more electrochemical cells. The cells use chemical reactions to create an electric charge. An electric current is an unbroken flow of electric charge through a pathway. An alkaline battery uses manganese dioxide, powdered zinc, and a paste called an electrolyte to create chemical reactions that produce an electric charge. Eventually the zinc or the electrolyte will be used up, and a charge can no longer be produced.

In the future, fuel cells might be used in place of some batteries. Fuel cells create electric current through chemical reactions that mix oxygen and hydrogen gases. Fuel cells run for as long as they have enough fuel. Fuel cells have been used in space since the 1960s.

Making Electricity

An electric generator is a machine that changes mechanical kinetic energy to electrical energy. This generator makes the electricity that powers your home.

Inside an electric generator, a loop of wire turns at great speed. The wire moves through a magnetic field. This produces an electric current in the wire. The energy to spin the wire can come from many sources, such as friction or moving wind.

Solar cells are made of semiconductors, such as silicon, and use sunlight to produce electricity. Sunlight strikes the cell and knocks electrons out of silicon atoms, and an electric charge starts to flow.

Electric Power Plants

The electricity that powers your home comes from a power plant. Almost all power plants use the same kind of electric generators, but the energy to run the generators can come from different sources.

Many power plants burn coal or other fossil fuels. These fuels heat water to create steam. The steam turns huge turbines. Turbines are like large fans. The spinning turbines run the electric generators.

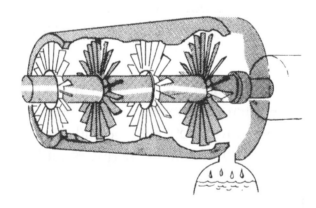

Hydroelectric power plants use the energy in running water to turn the turbines. Dams direct the water into the turbines. Nuclear power plants use nuclear fission to boil water and use the steam to turn the turbines.

Alternative sources of energy, like solar cells and solar panels, are good substitutes for fossil fuels that harm the environment. Solar materials generate energy from the sun. Similarly, geothermal power uses heat from Earth's interior. The spinning blades of a windmill can also run electric generators. But alternative energy sources can be limited. The necessary resources are not always available. For example, not all areas get a lot of wind and sun. In addition, solar panels are made with rare elements.

Name _____ Date _____

How Is Electricity Produced?

Match each definition to its term.

Definitions

Terms

____ **1.** a part of solar cells made of silicon

a. battery

____ **2.** a continuous flow of electric charge through a pathway

b. electric current

____ **3.** an object that contains one or more electric cells

c. solar cell

____ **4.** a device that runs by combining oxygen and hydrogen gas to cause an electrical current

d. fuel cell

____ **5.** a device that converts mechanical kinetic energy to electric energy

e. semiconductor

____ **6.** a device that uses the energy of the sun

f. electric generator

Write the kind of energy transformed to electricity by the devices below.

7. _____   8. _____   9. _____

Physical Science
Core Skills Science, Grade 5

10. Main Idea What is electric current?

_____

_____

11. Vocabulary Write a statement that defines the term *static electricity*.

_____

_____

12. Reading Skill: Summarize Describe how a generator produces electricity.

_____

_____

13. Critical Thinking: Apply Describe the advantages and disadvantages of using batteries to create electricity. Why do you think fuel cells were used on the space shuttle instead of batteries?

_____

_____

14. Inquiry Skill: Collaborate Work with classmates to research wind power, geothermal power, or another alternative energy source. Describe its benefits and drawbacks and how it may be used in the future.

_____

_____

15. Test Prep Fuel cells use _____ to produce electrical energy.

    A zinc and an alkaline electrolyte

    B mechanical energy

    C copper and zinc

    D hydrogen and oxygen

What Is an Electric Circuit?

Circuits

A circuit is a closed loop. An object in a circuit begins at a starting point, moves through the loop, and arrives back at the start. It does not backtrack at any time. Think about a water park ride. Boats start at a high point of the track. Water carries them down a path. Then boats travel back to the high point to pick up new riders. What would happen if part of the path was missing or blocked off? Or what if the motor that lifted the boats stopped working? The ride would stop. The boats could not finish their circuit.

The path for an electric current is called an electric circuit. A battery lifts the charges in the circuit to give them higher electric potential energy. Voltage is a measure of a battery's electric potential energy per unit charge.

A conductor is a material that carries electricity well. Most wires used in electric circuits are made of copper, which is a very good conductor. Water is also a very good conductor. Electricity passes easily through water, so keep electric machines away from water. If they get wet, you could get an electric shock.

Any time a new material is used to create an object that uses electricity, it is important to test its conductivity. One way to do this is to construct a circuit that includes the new material. If the material is not a conductor, the circuit will not be able to be completed. Electricity will be blocked, which means that a different material should be used. An insulator is a material that does not carry electricity very well. Plastic is a good insulator. This is why most wires are coated with plastic. Wood and air are also good insulators. They prevent a circuit from being completed.

A circuit may be closed or open. In a closed circuit, electric current passes through the conductor again and again. When plugged in, a string of lights is a closed circuit. In an open circuit, insulators block the path of the charge. The current stops.

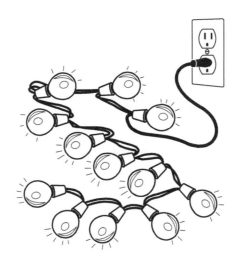

A switch can open or close a circuit. A switch is a simple part that moves. As it moves, it opens and closes a path for electricity. When the switch is closed, the circuit is closed. Electric current flows all the way around the circuit.

Series Circuit

In a series circuit, electricity follows just one path. If two or more light bulbs are connected to a battery along one path, they form a series circuit. All the bulbs share voltage from the battery. If one bulb is removed, the circuit opens and the electricity stops.

Parallel Circuit

In a parallel circuit, electric current can follow two or more different paths. If two or more light bulbs are connected to a battery and lined up in a row, the current follows a parallel circuit. It takes different paths to get to each bulb.

When you take a bulb away, only the path to that bulb is opened. The other bulbs stay lit. In a parallel circuit, the light bulbs do not share voltage from the battery. The circuits in your home are set up in parallel series. If you turn off a lamp, for example, other lights stay on.

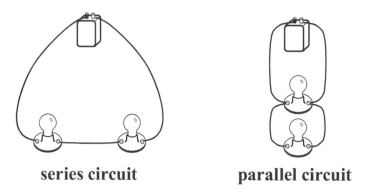

series circuit   parallel circuit

Electrical Safety

Be safe around electricity. Only plug electrical equipment into household outlets. Otherwise, you could get shocked! Electricity can also produce heat as a side effect. Lamps, electric wires, and other equipment can overheat. Fires can even start this way. The higher the current, the stronger the heat is.

Fuses and circuit breakers can stop circuits from overheating. Most homes use them. A fuse has a thin metal strip inside it. The strip is part of an electric circuit. The strip will melt if the current flowing to it gets too high. When this happens, the circuit opens.

A circuit breaker works a lot like a fuse. A circuit breaker has a switch instead of a metal strip. Too much current trips the switch, making the circuit open. You flip the switch to close the circuit. So, circuit breakers can be used again and again. Fuses must be replaced after they stop electricity just once. For this reason, most new homes use circuit breakers.

What Is an Electric Circuit?

Write answers to the questions on the lines below.

1. What is an electric circuit?

   _____

   _____

2. What does the voltage of a battery tell you?

   _____

3. What is a conductor?

   _____

   _____

4. What materials are good insulators?

   _____

   _____

5. What happens in a series circuit when one light bulb burns out?

   _____

   _____

6. Which type of circuit, a series circuit or a parallel circuit, would allow the light bulbs to burn brighter? Why?

   _____

   _____

   _____

7. **Main Idea** Why does an electric circuit have to be closed for it to work?

_____

_____

8. **Vocabulary** In your own words, define *parallel circuit*.

_____

_____

9. **Reading Skill: Draw Conclusions** You plug in a string of lights and none of them light up. You test the outlet and verify that it works. What might be the problem?

_____

_____

10. **Critical Thinking: Evaluate** What would you suggest to a person who complained about having to replace fuses all the time?

_____

_____

11. **Inquiry Skill: Record Data** How are series circuits and parallel circuits similar and different? Draw diagrams.

_____

_____

12. **Test Prep** Which of the following produces a voltage?

   A light bulb

   B battery

   C wires

   D a closed switch

Answer Key

What Are the Parts of a Cell? LS1.A (MIDDLE SCHOOL)

1. nucleus
2. a plant cell because it has a cell wall and chloroplasts
3. c   4. d   5. a
6. b   7. e
8. All living things are made of cells. Cells come from existing cells. A cell is the smallest unit of life.
9. Sample answer: The nucleus is the organelle that supervises activities in the cell.
10. Both make objects look much bigger than they really are. Light microscopes make objects appear 2000 times bigger; electron microscopes can make objects look 40,000 times bigger.
11. The presence of certain cell parts indicate whether it is a plant or animal cell.
12. Both enclose and protect the cell. A cell wall is rigid and is found only in plant cells; a cell membrane is flexible.
13. C

How Do Single-Celled Organisms Live? LS1.A (MIDDLE SCHOOL)

1. take in food; get rid of wastes; digest nutrients so they can use and store energy, grow, and reproduce
2. break down remains of dead plants, help produce and process some foods, help body digest food properly
3. diffusion: the movement of particles from an area of higher concentration to an area of lower concentration; osmosis: diffusion in which water passes through a cell membrane
4. budding
5. Both need water, food, and some way to get rid of wastes.
6. Sample answer: Osmosis is a type of diffusion in which water passes through a cell membrane.
7. The cilia might function to move the organism through water or to move food particles toward the organism.
8. It might kill some of the beneficial bacteria in your body.
9. Students' experiments should involve sealing a bag of sugar, water, and yeast so no air can reach the yeast.
10. A

How Are Cells Organized? LS1.A (GRADE 4)

1. Organ—group of related tissues that perform a specific function
2. Organ system—group of related organs that work together to perform a specific function
3. b   4. c   5. a
6. e   7. d
8. Capillaries connect arteries to veins.
9. Sample answer: Organs are made up of one or more kinds of tissues that perform certain functions.

10. Sample answer: circulatory system pumps blood through body; respiratory system moves air in and out of body
11. Vertebrates have skeletal systems, unlike invertebrates.
12. Sample answer: What does the cell nucleus do? How does muscle tissue change size and shape? How does the heart work? How does a fish use its nervous system? How tall can a tree grow?
13. B

How Do Plants Make Food? PS.3.D; LS1.C

1. photosynthesis   2. sugars
3. chloroplasts   4. grana
5. chlorophyll   6. blade
7. stomata   8. oxygen
9. carbon dioxide
10. oxygen, sugars
11. Sample answers: Chloroplasts are organelles in which photosynthesis takes place. Stomata are small openings in a leaf that let in carbon dioxide and release oxygen.
12. Sunlight hits chlorophyll. Water molecules split into hydrogen and oxygen. Hydrogen joins with carbon from carbon dioxide to make sugars. Oxygen is released. All living things need oxygen to live.
13. in the stem; the green color comes from chlorophyll
14. Monitor oxygen and carbon dioxide levels in two houses, one with many houseplants and one with few or no houseplants.
15. C

How Do Plants Move Materials? LS2.B

1. roots: roots   2. stem: tree trunk
3. leaves: leaves
4. root pressure, cohesion, and transpiration
5. They keep water in the roots.
6. Cohesion causes water and minerals to cling to each other, creating tension that moves water and minerals up the stem.
7. transpiration: evaporation pulls water from the leaves up the stem
8. Nonvascular plants do not have structures like leaves, stems, or roots. Vascular plants have these structures. Nonvascular plants cannot move food and water between plant parts, but vascular plants can.
9. Xylem and phloem are specialized tissues that move water, minerals, and food in plants. Xylem carries water and minerals upward. Phloem moves food downward.
10. It is a strip of tissue. It lies between the xylem and phloem. It is where xylem and phloem cells are made.
11. It would eliminate the pull from above, so water might not reach the leaves.

12. The plants would die because no water would reach the roots. The roots would have no water to push up the stem of the plant.
13. B

How Do Plants Reproduce? LS1.B (MIDDLE SCHOOL)

1. c   2. e   3. d
4. a   5. b
6. stamen   7. pistil   8. stigma
9. Angiosperms are the most numerous.
10. Sample answer: Gymnosperms have seeds and no fruits or flowers. Angiosperms are flowering plants.
11. They are all reproductive organs of plants. Seedless plants use sporangia to reproduce. Gymnosperms use cones, and angiosperms use flowers.
12. Bees and butterflies help plants reproduce by carrying pollen.
13. They have flowers that protect their reproductive parts and fruits that protect seeds. They produce seeds quickly.
14. A

What Are Biomes? LS2.A

1. tropical rain forests
2. Temperate rain forests
3. desert   4. tundra
5. Possible answers: Intertidal: crabs, snails; Near-Shore: kelp, otters; Open Ocean: algae, whales; Streams and Rivers: fish, beavers, birds; Ponds and Lakes: algae, insects, fish, plankton
6. climate and type of vegetation
7. a large group of similar ecosystems; tropical rain forests, temperate forests, grasslands, deserts, taiga, tundra
8. Summaries should include the type of climate and living things found in the biome.
9. Algae need sunlight to produce food. Sunlight doesn't penetrate deep ocean water.
10. land biomes in temperate regions
11. D

What Is a Food Web? LS1.C; LS2.A; LS2.B

1. sunlight   2. eating
3. Sample answers: Producer: grass; Primary consumer: caterpillar; Second-level consumer: bird; Third-level consumer: cat
4. decomposers   5. herbivore
6. carnivores   7. omnivores
8. oxygen   9. producers
10. from producers to consumers to decomposers
11. Food chain shows how energy flows from one organism to another; food web is all the food chains in an ecosystem.
12. Sample answers: producer: tree; herbivore: rabbit; carnivore: hawk; omnivore: human; decomposer: fungus

129

13. Other organisms would die because plants provide the energy at the bottom of the energy pyramid.
14. Food chains will vary but should show a producer at the beginning and the student at the end.
15. B

What Are Habitats and Niches? LS4.B (MIDDLE SCHOOL)
1. the area where an organism lives
2. A niche describes what an organism does in its habitat.
3. A sea turtle developed flippers to move through ocean water. The bird has a long, pointed beak to help it search for food among rocks on a beach.
4. a close, long-lasting relationship between two different organisms
5. Parasitism is a type of symbiosis. One organism benefits from living off the body of another organism, which is hurt.
6. lion eats zebra; zebra eats grass
7. Mutualism is a type of symbiosis. In mutualism, two organisms help each other.
8. Differences make their ability to survive better or worse; those with characteristics that help them will pass those characteristics to future generations.
9. Students may describe their niches as being in neighborhoods with houses and stores.
10. Sample response: Bees eat nectar from flowers and carry pollen to other flowers. Both benefit.
11. D

"What Are the Layers That Make Up the Earth? ESS2.A; ESS2.C
1. Answers vary, but may include mountains, volcanoes, and canyons.
2. nitrogen, oxygen, carbon dioxide
3. underground or in glaciers
4. Energy comes in and out, but matter does not.
5. Plants and animals live in the ocean.
6. The sun causes water to heat up, affecting temperature and climate.
7. geosphere, hydrosphere, atmosphere
8. geosphere: underground minerals and rocks, landforms; atmosphere: air; hydrosphere: water; biosphere: living things
9. Sphere can mean a round shape/object or can refer to one of Earth's four parts.
10. Most of the water is in oceans; the rest is in glaciers, underground, in the atmosphere, or in smaller bodies of water.
11. Answers may vary.
12. Answers may vary.
13. D

What Makes Up Earth's Surface? ESS2.A
1. fresh water
2. salt water
3. land
4. Mountain valleys
5. wide plains

6. Deep canyons, underwater mountains
7. ocean basin
8. location, shape, elevation
9. You can learn the shape and steepness of land.
10. continental shelf: forms edge of a continent; continental slope: forms side of a continent; continental rise: stretches out across ocean floor
11. There is much water but not much fresh water. Living things need fresh water to drink, so it is a valuable resource.
12. Both are flat and wide. Plateaus rise above their surroundings; plains are lower than their surroundings.
13. B

How Is Earth's Surface Worn Down and Built Up? ESS2.A (GRADE 4)
1. sediment
2. Erosion
3. Glaciers
4. sinkhole
5. landslides
6. the moving of sediment from one place to another
7. a huge deposit of lava rock with sloping sides
8. About 65 million years ago, huge sections of Earth's crust crashed into each other, pushing up the land and forming the mountains.
9. When corals die, their skeletons build up into a bumpy ridge called a reef.
10. They break rock down into sediment (weathering) and carry the sediment away (erosion).
11. Erosion wears down Earth by carrying away sediment; deposition builds up land by releasing sediment that has moved from one place to another. Examples will vary.
12. Ocean waves crash on the shore. They break down rock along coastlines. Waves drag sediment back and forth, which forms sand.
13. They form on the ocean floor.
14. The shape can tell you from which direction the wind carrying sediment traveled. The size can tell you how long the dune has been there.
15. B

What Is Earth's Structure? ESS2.A; ETS1.C
1. Both suggest that the Earth's interior is very hot.
2. crust, mantle, outer core, inner core
3. cracks in the Earth's crust between two rocks
4. because the epicenter is above the fault, where seismic waves are strongest
5. vibrations that run through the Earth during an earthquake
6. melted rock
7. pressure from the weight of surrounding rock on magma
8. lava, gas, ash
9. The rocks along these boundaries usually experience greater stress.

10. crust and upper mantle
11. Hot rocks under Earth's surface heat water; pressure forces the hot water up and out of the Earth, forming a geyser.
12. It is a hotbed where many volcanoes erupt with fire-like lava and where earthquakes occur.
13. Rocks can represent crust, and boards can represent mantle. The tub of water can represent flowing rock material under the mantle.
14. A

How Do People Use Resources and Soil? ESS3.C
1. natural resources
2. fossil
3. moving water
4. Nonrenewable resources
5. renewable
6. residual soil
7. nutrients
8. soil horizons
9. topsoil
10. windbreak
11. because the sun shines every day
12. Sample answer: A soil profile shows the various levels of the soil, from topsoil to bedrock.
13. Sample answer: solar power because it is available everywhere
14. on relatively flat land, where there are no hills to obstruct the flow of wind
15. The soil is likely not fully formed and may not have enough nutrients to grow healthy plants.
16. C

What Factors Affect Climate? ESS2.A
1. cold year round; snowy
2. mild or warm summers; mild or cold winters
3. warm; rains often
4. water vapor
5. water cycle
6. windward
7. leeward side
8. equator
9. El Niño
10. mountains, bodies of water, Earth's overall shape
11. moving streams of water caused by winds blowing on the ocean's surface
12. Bodies of water cause uneven heating, which causes land and sea breezes. Ocean currents move energy and water making climates warmer or colder.
13. Places along the equator absorb more energy, and ocean currents are warmer along the equator.
14. Tropical climates are warm and wet. Temperate climates can be mild or severe and dry or wet. Polar climates are very cold and snowy all the time.
15. C

How Are Weather Forecasts Made?
1. nitrogen and oxygen
2. troposphere
3. stratosphere
4. Maritime
5. continental
6. clouds and light rain
7. Radar
8. Satellites
9. troposphere, stratosphere, mesosphere, thermosphere
10. a large volume of air that has mostly the same temperature and moisture throughout; its properties depend on where it is formed

11. A cold front came through the area. Clouds formed and dropped heavy rain.
12. Radar images can warn people of the storm. Then people have time to prepare their homes or evacuate to a safer area.
13. They would understand general weather patterns better.
14. A

What Are Stars and Galaxies? ESS1.A; ESS1.B
1. by size, color, brightness, and temperature
2. is closer to Earth than other stars
3. size, brightness
4. constellation
5. Earth is rotating.
6. see other stars during the day
7. a huge system of stars held together by gravity
8. a spiral-shaped galaxy that contains the solar system
9. universe
10. stars, planets, and moons
11. Answers may vary.
12. The temperature would increase so that all living things would die.
13. Answers will vary.
14. D

What Causes Day and Night? ESS1.B
1. It rotates on its axis and revolves around the sun.
2. They spin around an axis.
3. One side of Earth has daytime while the other side has nighttime.
4. The Earth's axis is tilted.
5. Because Washington, D.C., is facing the sun, it must be daytime. It is also summer because Earth's axis is tilted toward the sun.
6. Earth is rotating.
7. rotate; it's spinning on its axis, not moving in a circular path
8. The lengths of days and nights are not always the same.
9. more hours of daylight; The South Pole tilts toward the sun.
10. Sample answer: You could hold a ball and move in a circle around a lamp.
11. C

What Causes Earth's Seasons? ESS.1B
1. revolves
2. winter
3. revolution
4. summer solstice
5. toward
6. winter solstice
7. autumnal equinox
8. day and night: Earth's rotation; seasons: Earth's tilt
9. solstice: a pole is tilted toward the sun—summer, winter; equinox: neither pole is tilted toward the sun—spring, fall
10. As Earth orbits the sun, its tilt causes the sun's rays to strike places differently, causing changing temperatures.
11. The North Pole is tilted toward the sun; the South Pole is tilted away from the sun.

12. The sun moves across Earth's sky, and its rising and setting makes it appear as though it is making a big loop around the Earth.
13. C

Why Does the Moon Have Phases? ESS.1B
1. c
2. e
3. g
4. a
5. d
6. b
7. f
8. lunar eclipse
9. The moon moves into Earth's shadow.
10. The period of the moon's rotation is the same as its revolution, so only one side is visible.
11. the visible areas of the lit side of the moon
12. waxing gibbous, full moon, waning gibbous, last quarter, waning crescent, new moon, waxing crescent, first quarter
13. Observe the moon to determine its current phase and work through the sequence.
14. Both occur only when the sun, moon, and Earth are aligned and when one passes into another's shadow.
15. A

What Orbits the Sun? ESS.1B (MIDDLE SCHOOL)
1. a system in space made up of the sun and all the bodies, like planets and moons, that revolve around it
2. the strong gravitational force of the sun
3. the part of a comet that begins to glow when it gets near the sun
4. nucleus
5. tail
6. A meteoroid is a piece of rock or metal that orbits the sun. A meteor is a streak of light formed when a meteoroid strikes Earth's atmosphere at high speed and burns up.
7. a central star; eight planets and their moons; thousands of asteroids, comets, meteoroids
8. Sample answer: An asteroid is made of rock, and a comet is made of dust, ice, and frozen gases.
9. Outlines will vary. They might reflect that there is one sun, eight planets, numerous moons, and thousands of asteroids.
10. Earth has an atmosphere in which most meteoroids burn up.
11. Sample answer: Do research on the Internet, in the library, or by asking an astronomer.
12. D

What Are Elements? PS1.A; PS1.A (MIDDLE SCHOOL)
1. f
2. g
3. a
4. b
5. c
6. e
7. d
8. elements
9. properties
10. atomic
11. metals, nonmetals, metalloids
12. Metalloids
13. electrons, protons, neutrons
14. element's name, chemical symbol, atomic number

15. Both are made of carbon atoms. Their atoms are arranged differently, so they have different properties.
16. whether the element is shiny or dull, whether it can be bent or stretched, and whether it conducts electricity
17. The number of electrons is the same as the number of protons, so a uranium atom has 92 electrons.
18. C

What Are Compounds? PS1.A (MIDDLE SCHOOL)
1. a substance made up of two or more elements that are chemically combined
2. One or more substances are changed into one or more different substances.
3. H_2O
4. It has 2 atoms of iron and 3 atoms of oxygen.
5. energy
6. Water is liquid at room temperature, dissolves many substances, and has a unique shape.
7. They cannot be broken down into other substances, and all matter is made up of elements.
8. Sample answer: A chemical formula is a description of the number and type of elements in a compound.
9. Both are pure substances and have specific chemical properties. Elements have atoms of only one element; compounds have atoms of more than one element.
10. Answers will vary but should explain that a compound is made of two or more chemically combined elements.
11. The water created a chemical reaction with each of the two substances and created two new compounds.
12. D

How Can Materials Be Identified? PS1.A
1. physical property
2. chemical property
3. matter
4. volume
5. density
6. liquid
7. gas
8. solubility
9. Conductivity
10. thermal
11. They can be used to identify different materials and to distinguish one material from another.
12. Density is the substance's mass per unit volume.
13. They are different materials because the boiling point is the same for all samples of the same material.
14. electrical conductivity: if lightning hits water, the electric charge could travel through it and cause injury
15. 3 cm × 2 cm × 2 cm = 12 cm3; 1 cm = 1 mL; volume = 12 mL
16. C

What Are Solutions and Mixtures? PS1.B
1. mixture
2. heterogeneous, homogeneous
3. properties
4. vary

131

Answer Key
Core Skills Science, Grade 5

5. solute, solvent
6. homogeneous
7. solute   8. metals
9. Solutions are mixtures in which particles are evenly mixed at the level of molecules. Other mixtures may have different amounts of material distributed unevenly.
10. The solvent is the material that the solute dissolves in. The solute in salt water is the salt, and the solvent is the water.
11. Yes, the composition is uniform.
12. She could strain the soup to remove solids.
13. 27 g + 9 g = 36 g
14. D

What Are the Three States of Matter?
PS1.A

1. state of matter   2. closely
3. solid   4. liquid
5. gas   6. a solid forms
7. Gas forms when energy is added to a liquid.
8. A solid changes into a gas.
9. A gas changes into a solid.
10. arrangement and movement of particles
11. Vaporization is the change from a liquid to a gas; condensation is the change from a gas to a liquid.
12. Raising a liquid's temperature will cause it to evaporate. Boiling is rapid evaporation, which happens at higher temperatures than evaporation.
13. Gas particles move freely and escape from open containers.
14. Measure the solid's volume in different-sized containers. If the volume stays constant, it has melted and become a liquid. If volume changes, it has sublimated and become a gas.
15. D

What Can Change an Object's Motion? **PS2.B**

1. Motion   2. force   3. inertia
4. direction   5. 25 mph   6. net force
7. newton   8. gravity   9. Friction
10. A force can be applied.
11. Velocity is a measure of speed, direction: 6 km/h heading west; acceleration is a measure of change in velocity: 3 m/s².
12. It may speed up, slow down, or change direction.
13. When a moving car stops suddenly, inertia keeps a person moving forward. The shoulder strap stops the person's body and keeps it from hitting what is in front of him or her.
14. 120 km/h
15. D

How Are Sounds Made?

1. Transverse wave
2. Longitudinal wave
3. perpendicular   4. parallel
5. compression   6. rarefaction
7. a   8. c
9. d   10. b

11. Sound waves are a type of mechanical wave created by vibrations. They travel as longitudinal waves.
12. Vibrations are rapid back-and-forth movements. A guitar string vibrates when it is plucked, producing sound.
13. Long exposure to very loud sounds can damage hearing.
14. Materials in the room can affect the quality of sound by absorbing or reflecting it.
15. Sound might be absorbed or reflected. Since the surface is hard, it is reflected, not absorbed.
16. B

What Are Some Properties of Light?

1. wavelength
2. any three of: visible light, radio waves, gamma rays, microwaves, infrared rays, ultraviolet rays, x-rays
3. electromagnetic radiation that humans can see
4. ultraviolet radiation
5. any three of: eyeglasses, contact lenses, cameras, microscopes, and telescopes
6. a curved piece of clear material that refracts light in a predictable way
7. Electromagnetic waves travel in a vacuum; mechanical waves can't.
8. Sample answer: Reflection and refraction are behaviors of light.
9. Light waves change speed when they pass from one material to another. If they strike material at an angle, the waves change direction. Examples will vary.
10. The light rays may not be coming together correctly. Adjusting the lens could focus the image.
11. Radio waves have the longest wavelength.
12. C

What Is Thermal Energy? **PS3.A**
(GRADE 4)

1. A source of heat strikes the ice cube, and thermal energy is produced. The thermal energy melts the ice cube.
2. Fahrenheit scale
3. Temperature is a measure of the average kinetic energy of particles within a material.
4. Heat is the movement of thermal energy from warmer parts of matter to cooler parts.
5. d   6. a   7. c
8. e   9. b
10. conduction: direct contact; convection: the flow of liquids or gases; radiation: electromagnetic waves
11. conduction: thermal energy is passed from particle to particle; convection: thermal energy is transferred through a moving medium
12. There would be more thermal energy in the tub because there are more particles in motion. Different amounts of water at the same temperature have different amounts of thermal energy.

13. Place it near a heat source and measure its temperature increase.
14. Because water freezes at 0°C, a water thermometer would be unable to measure temperatures lower than this.
15. C

How Is Electricity Produced? ETS1.A

1. e   2. b   3. a
4. d   5. f   6. c
7. wind   8. solar
9. geothermal
10. a flow of electric charge through a pathway
11. Static electricity is a force between nonmoving charges.
12. It converts mechanical kinetic energy into electrical energy.
13. Sample answer: Batteries are portable but don't last long. Fuel cells don't create waste.
14. Answers will vary but should show understanding of the energy source and describe details about its benefits and drawbacks.
15. D

What Is an Electric Circuit? ETS1.B

1. the pathway for an electric current
2. The voltage tells you the amount of electric potential energy of the battery.
3. a substance that carries electricity well
4. plastic, wood, air
5. When one light bulb in a series circuit goes out, electric current stops flowing.
6. parallel circuit; in a parallel circuit, all bulbs receive the full voltage from the battery
7. Electricity has to keep moving to form a current.
8. It has separate pathways wired for devices to use.
9. The lights are wired in series and one of them is broken.
10. You might suggest the person have a circuit breaker installed because it can be used again and again.
11. Both require a closed circuit. Series circuits allow electricity to flow on just one path, while in a parallel circuit electricity can flow on more than one path. Diagrams should be accurate.
12. B